THE LAW
AND THE PROPHETS

THE LAW
AND THE PROPHETS

A Study of the Meaning of the
Old Testament

E 70

WALTHER ZIMMERLI

Translated by R. E. Clements

HARPER TORCHBOOKS ❦ The Cloister Library
Harper & Row, Publishers, New York

The James Sprunt Lectures delivered at
Union Theological Seminary, Richmond, Virginia
1963

First HARPER TORCHBOOK edition published 1967 by
Harper & Row, Publishers, Incorporated
49 East 33rd Street
New York, N.Y. 10016.

Contents

Abbreviations

ANET	*Ancient Near Eastern Texts*, ed. J. B. Pritchard, 2nd. ed., Princeton, 1955.
BA	*The Biblical Archaeologist.*
BZAW	*Beihefte zur Zeitschrift für die Alttestamentliche Wissenschaft.*
BJRL	*Bulletin of the John Rylands Library.*
Ev.Th.	*Evangelische Theologie.*
MVAG	*Mitteilungen der Vorderasiatischen-Aegyptischen Gesellschaft.*
RSV	Revised Standard Version of the Holy Bible.
SBT	*Studies in Biblical Theology.*
ThR	*Theologische Rundschau.*
ThWzNT	*Theologisches Wörterbuch zum Neuen Testament*, ed. G. Kittel and J. Friedrich, Stuttgart, 1933–.
ThZ	*Theologische Zeitschrift.*
WdO	*Welt des Orients.*
ZAW	*Zeitschrift für die Alttestamentliche Wissenschaft.*

Note. The biblical references and quotations in this study follow as far as possible the text of the Revised Standard Version. Occasionally, however, it has been necessary to emend it slightly, in order to present the full meaning of the original.

Preface

THE Faculty of Union Theological Seminary in Richmond, Virginia, invited me to deliver the James Sprunt Lectures in the week of 3rd–10th March, 1963, on a theme chosen from the field of Old Testament studies. The six lectures given on 'The Law and The Prophets' were abbreviated from a series of eleven lectures given in Göttingen in the summer semester of 1962. These were delivered in preparation for the Sprunt Lectures, and appeared in German in 1963 under the title 'Das Gesetz und die Propheten', as No. 166–168 of the 'Kleinen Vandenhoeck Reihe' in Göttingen.

My wife and I recall with gratitude our warm reception in Richmond, the good discussions with the students, and the generous hospitality which we received from President Jones, from my Old Testament colleagues John Bright and James L. Mays, from Professors James E. Bear, Henry M. Brimm, Balmer H. Kelly and their wives, and also from other members of the Faculty.

I particularly wish to thank Dr. R. E. Clements of the Faculty of Divinity in Edinburgh, who has undertaken to prepare the text of the lectures in a form suitable for critical English ears. I wish also to express my sincere thanks to my friend Professor G. W. Anderson, in whose house in Edinburgh I made my first attempts to speak English before my departure for America. I am indebted to him for the hospitality of his home in October 1962, and for all his help in the preparation of this English edition.

Göttingen, 4th January 1965   WALTHER ZIMMERLI

I

Introduction

THE Old Testament is an alien factor in recent Protestant theology. Admittedly it is not directly rejected, for the method of the 'German Christians', with their catchphrase 'Abolition of the Old Testament', arouses an attitude of fear. The Old Testament is honoured, and its words are read from the pulpit, yet when the systematic theologian endeavours to unfold what the Christian faith is, and to describe it in its essential parts, then the Old Testament is chiefly an embarrassment. It may be used for the purpose of illustration, or even in order to illuminate the structure of the biblical message, but when it comes to explaining the particular content of the word of God, then the Old Testament message to Israel is ignored. The word of the Old Testament is regarded as a preliminary stage. It is considered as knowledge which is imperfectly refined and therefore not properly relevant, so that it can be left aside at the arrival of the Gospel. It may even be regarded as a book of 'law', standing in direct antithesis to the New Testament.

The same state of affairs is also seen in large areas of New Testament scholarship. Here the Old Testament is used and honoured as a background document, because of its manifold relationships to the New. It cannot be ignored because of the inseparable connection with the Old Testament of which the New is conscious, yet, when it comes to plain theological thinking about the understanding of the authentic word of God, then the Old Testament has to be silent. The situation can arise in which a hermeneutic, which attempts seriously to grasp the real content of the New Testament proclamation, no longer sees a need for the word and proclamation of the Old.[1]

The Old Testament scholar is not justified in levelling reproaches here. This situation which exists in systematic theology, and in the sphere of New Testament studies, reflects the embarrassment which also exists widely in the field of Old Testament scholarship. On the basis of recent research the study of the Old Testament has undergone an unprecedented widening of its horizons and of the material available for its use. Israel's historical environment has been illuminated in an unexpected manner, and new cultural traditions which throw light on the

---

[1] E. FUCHS, *Hermeneutik*, Bad Cannstatt, 1954.

message of the Old Testament have become known. This knowledge, however, has widened still further the gap between Israel and the New Testament. The central question of the unity of the message of both Testaments has dropped into the background, although according to their own claim they are witnesses of the revelation of the one God, who cannot have given two separate revelations of his will. The effort to understand the authoritative word of the Old Testament is often confused with an attempt to maintain conservative historical positions in literary criticism, in order to establish the credibility of individual historical statements of the Old Testament, or to establish an early date for the appearance of monotheism. This return to orthodox views about the literary origin of the Old Testament, or its historical trust-worthiness, or even the modernity of its ideas, has in reality little significance for the effort to understand its authentic theological message.

The fact that the dialogue between Church and Synagogue is no longer felt to be a burning necessity is related to this secondary position of the Old Testament in theology. If the Old Testament is not really important for the question of the understanding of the biblical message, then there is also no compelling necessity to enter into a true dialogue with Judaism, which claims and listens to the Old Testament as its scripture. A discussion about a book of secondary importance can easily be left aside. Yet such indifference would become unthinkable if the Old Testament were to be understood as a part of the authentic revelation of God to his people.

Old Testament scholarship faces the task of penetrating to a new understanding of the entire theological witness of this book, in the light of all the newly acquired literary-critical and historical knowledge about it. We cannot disregard these new insights, even though they must be repeatedly subjected to critical examination. It would be dishonest to long for the flesh-pots of Egypt. In the light of these new horizons, and with a clear understanding of the historical distance and differences which separate us from Israel, we must seek to understand what the message of the Old Testament is, and how far the Church was right in preserving this book alongside the New Testament. The goal of a theological study of the Old Testament must be to make clear to the New Testament scholar, and the systematic theologian, what its message is, so that its place in the total biblical, and systematic theological, account of revelation cannot be ignored.

The lectures presented here do not pretend to accomplish this task

as a whole, or to offer a definitive new result. However, even though
they end with an open question, they may be regarded as an attempt in
this direction. They seek initially to follow the clue given by the two
concepts with which the New Testament refers to the Old. They
endeavour to follow critically and historically what happened to the
entities characterized by these two concepts. In this way we believe that
the most recent period of scholarship brings us to the place in which the
theologically relevant question is raised anew, and these lectures are,
as a whole, governed by this question. It is hoped further that they will
serve the free brotherly dialogue of the Church with Israel, which both
have to undertake in the light of the Old Testament.

I. The Problem

NEAR the end of the Sermon on the Mount Jesus summarizes the command to his disciples with the well-known rule: 'So whatever you wish that men should do to you, do so to them.' To this rule there is added in Matthew vii. 12 the remark 'for this is the law and the prophets'. In a similar way we hear it again in Matthew xxii. 40, where Jesus answers the lawyer's question about the greatest commandment of the law. Referring to the commandments of love to God, and of love to one's neighbour, Jesus adds, 'On these two commandments depend all the law and the prophets'.

We feel immediately that this combination of the law and the prophets is a kind of formula, which can be used to sum up the whole of the Old Testament revelation. It is found also in a quite different context. In the quotations referred to the formula occurs in a context which deals with the commandments of the Old Testament. The law and the prophets give expression to the divine claim upon men. In Acts xxiv. 14 the formula is related rather to the content of faith. In defending himself before the governor Felix, Paul affirms: 'But this I admit to you, that according to the Way, which they call a sect, I worship the God of our fathers, believing everything laid down by the law or written in the prophets.' Here Paul speaks in his own defence, whereas in Acts xxviii. 23 the formula is used more challengingly in the report of his preaching in Rome. He explains to the Jews the Kingdom of God 'trying to convince them about Jesus both from the law of Moses and from the prophets'. There is a difference in the use of the expression here. 'The law and the prophets' is not only a report of what has been done and spoken in former days, but together they represent a message of hope for the future announcing events of a time still to come. So Matthew xi. 13, speaking of John the Baptist, openly declares, 'All the prophets and the law prophesied until John'. It is not by accident that 'the prophets' are here put at the beginning of the formula, which is understood as a promise of things to come. This promise always contains a 'not yet', which is sharply underlined in Luke xvi. 16, where it is formulated quite tersely, 'The law and the prophets were until John; since then the good news of the kingdom of God is preached'. When Paul, in the key sentence of Romans iii. 21

5

speaks about the righteousness of God, which has been manifested apart from law through faith in Jesus Christ, and says that the law and the prophets bear witness to it, he means that the witness of that former time, which Luke regards as having passed, gains a new relevance through Christ and his gospel.

In the passages which we have cited from the New Testament it is apparent that we have stirred up many questions. Does the entity which is designated by the formula 'the law and the prophets', or 'the prophets and the law', exercise a claim upon men, or is it in the nature of a creed which explains what they are to believe? Alternatively are 'the law and the prophets' to be understood as a document of promise, the importance of which does not lie in itself, but in its foretelling of events which are yet to come?

We shall not answer all of these questions immediately. For the moment they can be laid aside in the hope that later we shall find some answers for them. Our initial task is much simpler. First we must ask what is the concrete meaning of the formula. Secondly we must ask why this formula is set out in the way it is. Thirdly we may raise the questions whether some deeper problem lies hidden behind the two notions 'the law and the prophets'.

First, what exactly does the formula 'the law and the prophets' include? Acts xxviii. 23 showed a fuller formulation when it spoke about 'the law of Moses and the prophets'. We also hear Philip saying to Nathaniel in John i. 45, 'We have found him of whom Moses in the law, and also the prophets wrote, Jesus of Nazareth, the son of Joseph'. Furthermore we can see that instead of speaking of the law it is possible simply to speak of Moses, so that the idea of law is replaced by the mention of Moses. Twice we hear in the parable of the rich man and Lazarus that the brothers of the rich man did not need an explicit warning; 'They have Moses and the prophets; let them hear them' (Luke xvi. 29), and again later on (verse 31), 'If they do not hear Moses and the prophets, neither will they be convinced if some one should rise from the dead.' In his apology before Festus Paul says, 'I stand here testifying both to small and great, saying nothing but what the prophets and Moses said would come to pass' (Acts xxvi. 22). Of the one who rose from the dead, Luke reports that he spoke to the disciples on the Emmaus road and 'beginning with Moses and all the prophets, he interpreted to them in all the scriptures the things concerning himself' (Luke xxiv. 27).

This last reference shows very clearly that 'Moses' as well as 'the prophets' means a collection of scriptures, and not merely some oral tradition, or code of laws preserved by oral tradition. 'Moses', or 'the law', evidently refers to the whole collection of books which can be found in the English Bible under the name of the five books of Moses. It obviously designates those books which begin in Genesis, the first book of Moses, with the creation of the world. After the primeval history, the beginnings of which gave to the book the name of Genesis (origin of the world), there follow the tragic stories of the Fall, of Cain and Abel, the Flood, and the beginning of the history of the nations in the account of the Tower of Babel. The narrative then narrows to give the history of the patriarchs, Abraham, Isaac and Jacob. Then the book of Exodus related the beginning of the history of the people of Israel, their liberation from Egypt, the house of bondage, and their encounter in the desert with God who gave to them their laws. In the second half of the book of Exodus, and in the books of Leviticus and Numbers, which describe further the wandering through the desert, we find a long account of the divine legislation for Israel, God's own people. The fifth book of Moses is set at the conclusion of the wandering through the desert, where Moses explains once more the entire law in an extensive valedictory address strongly admonitory in tone. Deuteronomy, and the whole collection of the Pentateuch, the five books, ends with the description of Moses' death. All that is 'Moses' is 'the law'.

The first part of the Old Testament is easily intelligible to the reader of the Bible. This is not the case with its second part, the prophets. We readily assume that this comprises those books which appear in the English Bible as the last section of the Old Testament writings under the names of individual prophets. Yet in the Hebrew canon of the Old Testament the collection of writings known as 'the Prophets' includes more than this, covering also most of what are usually termed the historical books. It is divided into two parts, the Former and the Latter Prophets, although these actual titles do not appear before the eighth century A.D. The whole collection follows immediately on the five books of the Pentateuch, so that we must bring them together with this first part of the canon. They follow directly the collection which tells the history of Moses and his time. The book of Joshua tells about the invasion by Israel of the land of Canaan, and the book of Judges describes the first period of Israel's dwelling in the land. This is the age in which charismatic leaders arose when Israel was oppressed by enemies. The two books of Samuel show how Israel decided to have a king at the time of the Philistine oppression, and then proceed to narrate the histories of Saul and David. The two books of Kings then sketch the following history of the united kingdom under Solomon, and the history of the two separated kingdoms up to their dissolution in the time of the Assyrian and Neo-Babylonian hegemony. When we compare this series of books with the series of books in our Bible, we see that in the 'Former Prophets' of the Hebrew canon there are omitted the books of Ruth, Esther and the whole of the work of the so-called Chronicler. This latter comprises the two books of Chronicles with Ezra and Nehemiah.

The second part of the canon of the Hebrew Bible combines these Former Prophets with the Latter Prophets, which appear at the end of the Old Testament in the English versions. Here also, however, there are some slight variations, as the Latter Prophets of the Hebrew Bible consist only of the three major prophets: Isaiah, Jeremiah and Ezekiel, with the book of the Twelve. The books of Daniel and Lamentations are missing in this part of the canon.

Where then are the remainder of the books of our Old Testament to be found? This includes those poetic books which appear in our Bible between the historical and the poetic books, and also those books which are omitted in the collection of the Former and Latter Prophets. In the Hebrew canon all of these are collected in a large third section of the canon under the rather colourless title, the Writings. In Luke xxiv. 44 Christ reminds his disciples that everything must be fulfilled which is 'written about me in the law of Moses and the prophets and the psalms'. Only here in the New Testament do we find an allusion to this last part of the Old Testament canon, which at that time does not seem to have been clearly defined. Along with the Psalms this section now contains also the poetic books of Proverbs and Job, the five Megilloth, or Festival Scrolls, of Song of Songs, Ruth, Lamentations, Ecclesiastes and Esther, together with the apocalyptic book of Daniel and the work of the Chronicler.

Our second question arises here. How did this striking arrangement of the Hebrew canon arise? In this strange arrangement of Law, Prophets, Writings can we discern a clear principle at work? Obviously the Jews of Alexandria felt the need to find some better arrangement and order. Through the Greek Septuagint and the Latin Vulgate the division of historical, poetic and prophetic books came into our translation of the Bible. In this grouping there is a literary interest which is completely lacking in the arrangement of the Hebrew Bible.

The explanation of this strange arrangement of the Hebrew canon is to be found in the way in which it developed. Its three parts have not been combined by means of a systematic reflection on the question of the best arrangement of the Old Testament books. The Old Testament canon has developed through supplementation during a process of historical growth. The three parts of the Hebrew Bible have grown like annual rings on a tree, so that in particular phases the whole of the canon was formed step by step. The five books of Moses form the historical nucleus of the whole collection, and a comparison with the Samaritan canon shows clearly that at one time only these books of Moses possessed the authority of holy scripture. The Samaritan community, which may have separated from the Jewish community around 300 B.C., is found in Palestine up to this day, and until today they acknowledge only the books of Moses as holy scripture. Their canon does not include prophetic writings, nor the writings of the third part of the Hebrew canon. The Samaritans had no reason to change radically the canon as it existed at the time of their secession. On the contrary they claimed to be the true community of Israel built upon the old solid foundation of Israel which had its centre at Shechem. At the time of their separation from Judaism the Pentateuch alone was evidently holy scripture. At the most it is possible that the prophetic writings were beginning to be honoured at this time, and the Samaritan reserve against this innovation was a mark of their traditional orthodoxy.

The twofold formula of the canon given in the New Testament indicates a second stage in its formation. The prophetic books were now added to the books of Moses. The third stage in the growth of the canon begins to appear when Luke xxiv. 44 mentions the Psalms in addition to the Law and the Prophets. (Is this also the case in Luke xxiv. 27?) A little earlier than this Philo, in referring to the *Therapeutae*, mentions that when they went off into solitude they took with them, 'laws and words prophesied by prophets and psalms, and the other writings by which knowledge and piety can be increased and improved'.[1] In Philo we hear the voice of Alexandrian Jewry, which is also heard as early as the end of the second century B.C., in the mouth of the grandson of Jesus Sirach (Ecclesiasticus), who translated the work of his grandfather into Greek. In the foreword to his translation he mentions his grandfather's study of 'the law, the prophets and the other books inherited from the fathers'. In general the Alexandrian Jews proceeded more quickly and more freely in widening the canon than did those of Palestine.

[1] PHILO, *De Vita Contemplativa*, Sec. 25.

Finally the Hebrew canon was fixed in a synod at Jamnia in the beginning of the second century A.D. We know little about this synod, although it is the occasion on which the Palestinian Jews limited their canon to the form of the Hebrew Bible as it has been handed down to us today. The limits of this Jewish canon are narrower than those in the Alexandrian collection of sacred scriptures. The books which make up the so-called Apocrypha were omitted. Rabbinic Judaism therefore came to call the threefold canon, the Law, the Prophets and the Writings (Heb. *Torah, Nebi'im, Ketubim,* abbreviated by its initials to *Tenach*).

Our concern here, however, is not with the history of the formation of the canon, and the controversies connected with it, but is limited to the twofold formula; the Law and the Prophets. This limitation is justified in that it is only these two headings which have a particular theological signification, whilst the subsequent fixing of the canon did not go beyond giving to its third part the colourless designation, the Writings. We are entitled, therefore, to concentrate our attention upon the two significant terms by which the New Testament describes the Old Testament canon, and to ask what deeper meaning is to be found in the combination of these two specific terms, the Law and the Prophets.

In doing this we approach the third question which was outlined at the beginning of this lecture, and which leads us to the real problem of the whole series of lectures. Does the designation of the Old Testament by the twofold formula, the Law and the Prophets, contain some deeper problem, and have a more profound significance for the real understanding of the whole Old Testament? Up to now all that we have discovered is that a particular history underlies the formation of this complex term. We now proceed to examine the true meaning of these two terms, and to ask what their content is.

The short summaries of the collections of biblical writings which are designated as the Law and the Prophets showed clearly that these two terms bring together very complex literary materials, and characterize them by a single heading. If we begin with the Law we find combined in the five books of Moses very different elements, beginning with the origin of the world and continuing with the history of Israel. In this narrative different poems are inserted. There is the boastful song of Lamech in Genesis iv. 23 f., and Exodus xv contains the song of Miriam, delivered on the shore of the Red Sea, and a song of Moses. A further song of Moses is found in Deuteronomy xxxii. We have collections of sayings about the tribes in the Blessing of Jacob (Gen. xlix) and the

Blessing of Moses (Deut. xxxiii). These poems appear side by side with a good deal of legal material, beginning in the book of Exodus, and continuing through to Deuteronomy. By way of simplification all of this literature is collected under the single heading of law. Behind this designation there undoubtedly lies the correct realization that from Exodus to Deuteronomy a large amount of legal material is assembled. In a more cautious manner we can speak of a great deal of instruction given to the people of Israel through Moses. This instruction tells the people what is required of them in their cultic and social life. At the same time it is plain that the catchword 'law' gives a certain interpretation to the material. It is seen from a certain perspective, so that what is collected in the five books of Moses is relevant for Israel's faith because it is law.

At this point I should like to make a remark that may keep us from jumping too hastily to false conclusions. The word law has a long history, and in our minds it immediately evokes certain associations. The lawyer thinks of the power of the state which enables him to enact laws. The man who reads the New Testament, and who understands something about Pauline theology, combining it with ideas drawn from the theology of the Reformation, is inclined to regard law as something opposed to the divine promise, and so as the opposite of the Gospel. Law is a demand upon us, and so is bad and pernicious, whilst the Gospel is a saving gift which spreads mercy. In our biblical context the first notion, that law is a concern of the state, has had the ground cut from under it, since M. Noth[1] has clearly demonstrated that Mosaic law has nothing to do with the law of the state. Against the second way of regarding law we must interject the protest of Martin Buber in his book *Two Types of Faith*.[2] He holds that the interpretation of law as a demand, and as a condemnation, is a consequence of the translation of the Hebrew *torah* by the Greek *nomos*, where the latter does not adequately represent the meaning of the original. In the theology of von Rad[3] we find the same thesis. It is better, therefore, to put this association aside for the time being. Any truth that it contains will become apparent in the course of our investigation.

We limit ourselves here to a very short provisional remark. The word law corresponds to the Hebrew *torah*, which means primarily a directive regarding a priestly or cultic matter,[4] as for example in the

[1] See below page 45.   [2] M. BUBER, *Two Types of Faith*, London, 1951.
[3] See below pages 46 ff.
[4] J. BEGRICH, 'Die priesterliche Tora', *BZAW* 66 (1936), pp. 63–88.

sacrificial laws of Leviticus vi ff. Haggai ii. 10 ff. shows, however, that
it was also the technical term for information given by a priest to laymen who came to him for guidance. In this case the priest informs the
layman whether holy meat, i.e. sacrificial meat, can make bread or soup
holy when it touches them, or whether any kind of food is defiled
through contact with what is unclean. In the course of time use of the
word *torah* was extended. The whole address of Moses in Deuteronomy
which declares the order of Israel's life after the conquest of the promised land, is described as *torah*. In this instance *torah* is the comprehensive guidance on right behaviour in the land which God has given.
At an even later date the word came to encompass the whole corpus of
the Pentateuch. At this point the proclamation of God's will, with its
claim upon the entire people of Israel, has become the central feature.
We cannot decide here, however, whether this claim pardons man or
threatens him. In the Greek translation the word was not only trans-
ferred into a new linguistic context, but it doubtless received also a new
accentuation. In Greek thought *nomos* is a word which also denotes
the order of the state, a meaning which is completely absent in the
Hebrew *torah*.

Beside the Law we find the Prophets. Here also we see immediately
that we have to do with a simplification of more complicated facts by
the grouping together of various materials under a single heading. The
second part of the canon, like the first, begins with a simple narrative
account. It describes the conquest of the land and the period of the
judges before an Israelite state had come into being. We may well be
surprised why all this narrative is given under the title 'the Prophets'.
Only when the history of Samuel begins, and the birth of the Israelite
kingdom comes into view, does the term 'prophet' (Heb. *nabi'*) begin
to emerge clearly. In the history of David which follows, and more
clearly still in the accounts of the later kings, prophets come to play
an important role. In the books of the latter prophets they then
dominate the books as a whole.

In this second part of the canon as well, therefore, we see that its
title is both a summary and an interpretation. We find a theological
statement, just as we did in the interpretation of the first part of the
canon. To the claim that the normative divine will is to be heard in the
torah given by Moses, we now have the further assertion that the
authentic word of God is also to be found in a second source, the
person of the prophet. The word of God is the way in which God is
active in and through the prophet. We must keep in mind that the

relationship of the Prophets to the Law did not come about through any deliberate systematizing principle, but was rather a consequence of historical development. In Israel, after the divine instruction had been given by the commandments of the law, however this actually came to be determined historically, the fact of prophecy occurred with such force that Israel could not ignore it. The words of the prophets had to be collected, and, because of their importance, they came to be considered parallel to the Law as a second, and no less valid, authority.

The Law and the Prophets means much more than simply the putting together of two subject headings, which in fact have no final authority. They are more than mere notions used to bring some order into the variety of the traditions. On the contrary, to these two factors the whole tradition is subordinated in a very forcible way, and the third part of the canon never attained a similar authority to that which they enjoyed. Through them, therefore, a very important theological insight, or perhaps we should say more cautiously, a theological interpretation, is given, which we must listen to and consider.

However, as soon as we do so a new question arises very pertinently. What is the relationship between these two ways in which God's utterance is given to men? Simply to establish that in putting the Prophets alongside the Law, the Old Testament canon expresses God's way with his people is to leave our task unfinished. Theological thought has to examine the inner relationship of these two manifestations of God's revelation. Just as in New Testament times Christians had to ask what the relationship was between the Holy Spirit, which was given after the divine revelation in Christ, and this event itself, so also Old Testament theology has to ask what significance attaches to . the gift of the prophetic word after the revelation of the divine law to Israel. What is the inner relationship of these two phenomena of divine revelation in the Old Testament?

Theoretically the relationship between the two could be of several kinds. Theological examination may discover that the Law and the Prophets are identical. What was first said through the law was subsequently revealed anew through the prophetic word in the time of the prophets. Or it might be seen that the prophetic word was clearly subordinated to the law, so that the prophets were simply interpreters of the law at a later time. But it is also conceivable that the prophets brought something new, which needed to be added to the law, or even that what the prophets proclaimed led to an inner crisis in the law, so that they shattered the existing understanding of it.

If we consider the New Testament references to the Law and the Prophets, then we can establish that nowhere is there a sign of tension between the two. The formula holds together without difficulty, and the connection of the two words expresses a single reality and gives witness to the one will of God revealed in the Old Testament.

If we then go on to ask how this one will of God, revealed by the Law and the Prophets, is to be understood, then the passages in Matthew give a clear answer. Jesus affirms in Matthew v. 17 that he did not come to abolish the law and the prophets, but to fulfil them. When verse 18 adds that until the end of heaven and earth not an iota or a dot will pass from the law, then this addition clearly shows that 'the Law and the Prophets' can be summarized under the single heading of 'the Law'. Matthew vii. 12; xxii. 40 and Luke xvi. 29, 31 point in the same direction. In this regard we must notice that beside the twofold formula 'the Law and the Prophets' we also find in the New Testament a singular designation of the Old Testament simply as 'the Law'.[1] We can understand this singular designation of the Old Testament from the history of the formation of the canon. In the first phase of its formation, as is proved by the case of the Samaritan canon, only the Pentateuch was acknowledged as sacred scripture by the Jewish community. From this the prophets could easily be regarded as no more than commentators on the law.

This is what we find in Jewish tradition. The Babylonian Talmud (Megilloth 14a) says, 'Forty-eight prophets and seven prophetesses have prophesied to the Israelites and neither have they diminished anything nor have they added anything to what is written in the torah except the recital of the roll of Esther'.[2] Rabbi Joshua ben-Levi, on the other hand, says that Moses had already spoken all the words of the prophets and 'all that was prophesied afterwards comes from the prophecy of Moses' (Midrash Exodus Rabba xlii. 8 on xxxii. 7).[3] The same understanding, that what the prophets declared derives from Mosaic times, and from the same source as the law, is further expressed by Rabbi Isaac (c. A.D. 300), who interprets Isaiah as saying, 'On the day on which the torah was given on Sinai I was present, and I received this prophecy. But now God has sent me and his spirit (Is. xlviii. 16). Until today I was not authorized to prophesy' (Midrash Exodus Rabba xxviii. 6 to xix. 3).[4]

The development in Judaism continues in this direction. As a conse-

---

[1] E.g. Rom. iii. 19; 1 Cor. xiv. 21.   [2] Cf. *ThWzNT*, VI, p. 818.
[3] Ibid.   [4] Ibid.

quence of the subordination of the Prophets to the Law the former receive a lower evaluation. Luke iv. 17 and Acts xiii. 15 mention the reading of the Law and the Prophets during the Sabbath worship. The actual arrangement of the readings shows very clearly that the section of the Prophets, the so-called *haphtara* (meaning 'what closes the reading of the scripture') stands after the reading of the *torah*, which always holds the first place. The reading of the scrolls of the *torah* is highly honoured, and is subject to careful restriction, whilst the rules prescribed for the reading of the *haphtara* are relatively lax. They allow a reading from the scroll of a single prophet, or from scrolls which contain only the particular sections from the Prophets which are to be read. After the invention of printing the prophetic texts were allowed to be read in the synagogue from printed books, which is not the case with the *torah*. For the reading of the *torah* a number of men have to be called, while the *haphtara* may be read by only one man, who is also obliged to read also a passage of the *torah* lest the reading of the Prophets should be given a higher honour. Minors also have the right to read the Prophets, but are strictly forbidden to read the *torah*.[1] All these regulations make quite clear that the Prophets stand in the shadow of the *torah* and are regarded as inferior to it.

In the New Testament we can discern that there is a different line of thought. In Matthew xi. 13 it is stated that the law and the prophets prophesied until the time of John, and according to John i. 45 Moses wrote about the Christ in the law, as also did the prophets (so also Luke xxiv. 27; Acts xxvi. 22). In Romans iii. 21 Paul says that the law and the prophets witness to the righteousness of God through faith in Jesus Christ, and it seems that in all these instances both the law and the prophets are understood from the starting point-of the prophets, without any feeling of a tension arising between the two.

This unity of the Law and the Prophets, without a noticeable tension between the two, existed also in the Christian Church of a later time, regardless of which received the greater emphasis. Starting from the Law, the task of the prophets could be understood as a revelation of law, or by beginning with the Prophets, the law could be understood in the light of the promises made from the beginning in the stories of Adam and Cain. A quotation from Luther's preface to the prophets may illustrate this: 'What can we say about the other books of the prophets and the histories? Answer: they are in nothing different from

[1] I. ELBOGEN, *Der Jüdische Gottesdienst in seiner geschichtlichen Entwicklung*, Leipzig, 1913, pp. 174–84.

Moses. Together they fulfil the office of Moses, and guard against false prophets, lest they should lead the people astray to works. The prophets enabled them to remain in the authority of Moses and in the knowledge of the law'.[1]

Thus in the lectures which follow we must examine the relationship of the Law to the Prophets from the standpoint of our modern knowledge of the Old Testament. Behind this question, however, there arises even more acutely the more comprehensive question of how the Old Testament as a whole, which embraces the two fundamental manifestations of God's revelation; the Law and the Prophets, is to be understood.

[1] M. LUTHER, *Vorrede auf das Alte Testament*, Weimarer Ausgabe, Bibel VIII 28.

II. Wellhausen's Thesis:
The Law is later than the Prophets

LUTHER, whose words about the prophets we have already referred to, understood the message of the Bible as a message of promise (*promissio*). He points out in his preface to the Old Testament that this promise is already found in the Old Testament. 'There are in the Old Testament, besides the laws, many promises and words of grace by which the holy patriarchs and prophets were kept under the law through faith in Christ, as are we.'[1] In the proclamation of law and promise the prophets stand beside Moses.

In the period of orthodoxy which followed, the emphasis was slightly different. Instead of 'promise' it became preferable to use the term 'pure doctrine', and the prophetic office came to be regarded in this context. This can be seen already in the writings of Melanchthon. 'In the Old Testament', he says, 'the prophets are called teachers (*doctores*), who were appointed directly by God in order to purify the doctrine (*ad repurgandam doctrinam*), and above all to explain the promise of the Messiah, and to give political advice. They were equipped with the testimony of miracles, in order to establish with certainty the divinity of their teaching (*doctrinam eorum*).'[2]

The age of rationalism continued along this line, except that the question of *doctrina* was no longer understood as an ecclesiastical concern, but as the pursuit of truth on the basis of general human reason. In this regard Spinoza's *Tractatus theologico-politicus* (1670) is very instructive, and shows at the same time, how the law and the prophets could be regarded on a similar level, without any tension arising between them. In the first three chapters of this tractate Spinoza examines prophecy. In the fourth chapter he talks about the divine law in general, and goes on in chapter five to deal with particular religious customs. Chapters 6–20 then deal with more particular questions of the Old Testament. Here Spinoza says, 'I found that the explicit teaching of the Bible contains nothing which is not agreeable to natural thought,

---

[1] M. LUTHER, *Vorrede auf das Alte Testament*, Weimarer Ausgabe, Bibel VIII 12.
[2] MELANCHTHON, *Corpus Reformatorum*, 21, p. 1099.

or which contradicts it. Furthermore I found that the prophets in particular have only taught quite simple things, which anyone can understand easily.'[1] The true divine law, which gives real happiness to man
is innate in him, and is the common property of the human spirit. On
the other hand the concrete prescriptions of the law are concerned with
the temporal welfare of the state. The prophets, however, were not
endowed with a superior spirit, but only with a more vivid imagination.
They saw visions, and they heard the word of God. The inner certainty of their preaching was not that of a mathematical proof, as
Spinoza sought for his own philosophy,[2] but was a moral conviction.
The vitality of their imagination gave an immediate assurance to their
experiences, and, as Melanchthon argued, signs were a proof of their
credibility. It is also noteworthy from the modern psychological viewpoint to see how Spinoza explained the individuality of the different
prophets. He saw the particular colour of each prophet's message as
entirely dependent on the subjective disposition of the prophet. Spinoza
says, 'When the prophet was a farmer he saw oxen, cattle etc.; when a
soldier, he saw captains and armies; when a courtier, he saw the king's
throne and such like.' According to Spinoza the character of the preaching depended also on the prophet's temperament. 'When the prophet
had a cheerful disposition, victory, peace and whatever pleases people
were revealed to him, for the imagination of cheerful people is very
often full of pleasant things. On the other hand wars, judgment and all
kinds of misfortune were revealed to a prophet with a melancholy
character.' Also in the matter of style the background of the prophet
can be recognized: 'When the prophet was a man of taste, then also he
heard the thoughts of God with tasteful perception; if he were of a confused disposition, then he heard them in a confused way.' From this
the contradictions and differences can be understood. 'Depending on
their disposition the prophets were, therefore, more suited to receive
one kind of revelation rather than another.'[3]

In this way Rationalism sought after eternal truth. Admittedly it
recognized also the transitory, but only the eternal had significance,
and this was the same both in the law and the prophets.

Not until the nineteenth century did the unified conception of the
law and the prophets begin to break up. At this point we may mention

---

[1] *Tractatus theologico-politicus*, Eng. trans., London, 1862, pp. 26 ff.

[2] His philosophical system appeared under the title *Ethica More Geometrico
Demonstrata*.

[3] B. SPINOZA, *Tractatus theologico-politicus*, p. 55.

Herder, even though he did not write a separate essay on the prophets. His two-volume work *Vom Geist ebraischer Poesie* began to appear in 1782, and thus stands at the threshhold of the nineteenth century. In it he dealt with the prophets, and saw in them artists who spoke in poetic inspiration, which is not the same as a supernatural inspiration. According to Herder they were to be regarded not as representatives of a group, but as individual personalities. We can see in this the romantic concept of personality, which recognized and preserved the mystery of the individual, and regarded it as incommunicable to others except through sympathetic understanding. 'Each of these holy men of God spoke under the impulse of the Holy Spirit as an individual, whether as the leader of the people, or as the spokesman of the will of God to a particular city or age.'[1] Herder himself was indifferent to the problem of defining the exact historical situation of the prophecies, but it is easy to see that his view gave a strong impetus towards understanding the actual individual historical figure. As far as the prophets as a whole are concerned, Herder regarded them as still in line with Moses. 'Moses provided for the restoration of sacred song in times of national decay through the law of prophecy. The prophets were the successors of Moses, who applied and renewed his law in periods of national decline. Some of them were gifted men, being brilliant orators and creative poets.'[2]

We must now turn in greater detail to the work of Heinrich Ewald. His two-volume work *Die Propheten des Alten Bundes* (1840–1)[3] was published before the great critical transformation in the study of Israelite history, for which Ewald's greatest pupil, J. Wellhausen, strove so hard in his writings. Nevertheless it represents a great personal achievement, which pointed the way for future study. In a speech delivered in 1901 Wellhausen said of Ewald's book on the prophets, 'This is Ewald's exegetical masterpiece. The prophets were congenial to him, and he penetrated more deeply into their nature than any of his predecessors.'[4]

I cannot resist saying a few words about Ewald's life. He was born in 1803 in Göttingen as the son of a poor weaver, and began in 1820 to

[1] Quoted from L. DIESTEL, *Geschichte des Alten Testamentes in der Christlichen Kirche*, Jena, 1869, p. 762.   [2] L. DIESTEL, op. cit., p. 762.

[3] Published in two volumes 1840–1. The second edition appeared in three volumes 1867–8. The first edition is quoted here.

[4] J. WELLHAUSEN, *Festschrift zur Feier des hundertfünfzigjährigen Bestehens der Königlichen Gesellschaft der Wissenschaften zu Göttingen, Beiträge zur Gelehrtengeschichte Göttingens*, Berlin, 1901, p. 73.

study classical philogy and oriental languages, receiving his doctor's degree at the age of nineteen. After a year of teaching in Wolfenbüttel he became a tutor in the University of Göttingen, and in 1827 was elected as extraordinary professor, become ordinary professor in 1831. In 1837 he was dismissed from the university for being one of the seven professors, the *Göttinger Sieben*, who protested against the suspension of the 1833 state constitution by the Hanoverian king Ernst August. In 1838 he was called to Tübingen where he remained until 1848, when he was called back to Göttingen. He was a member there of the faculty of philosophy until 1867, when he was dismissed from it because he refused to take an oath of loyalty to the Prussian king, after the conquest of Hanover by the Prussians. In 1868, after the publication of a political tract, he was also forbidden to lecture any longer. After he had been elected to the German parliament he was three times charged with insulting the king. In his personal life he was a rather awkward man, but in academic and political affairs he was a tough protagonist, and until the last days of his life he remained a scholar of exceptional creative ability and power. Through all his struggles he became in the end a rather lonely person. On a portrait of Ewald, in Wellhausen's possession, there is written in the latter's handwriting the words spoken of Ishmael in Genesis xvi. 12, 'his hand against every man and every man's hand against him'. In Wellhausen's commemorative address referred to above, which is a masterly example of devout gratitude and sober criticism on the part of a pupil, the account of Ewald's life concludes with the sentence, 'He died on May 4th, 1875, in conflict with the world, but in peace with God.'[1]

Ewald dealt with the prophets in the work to which we have referred, and one of the distinctive features of his treatment is that he gave a complete translation of his own, to which he added a running commentary. This combination is a characteristic of Ewald's whole method. He does not work from a general concept of prophecy to the study of an individual prophet, but listens attentively to the individual prophet, and seeks to understand what he has to say to him as a whole. He does, however, in his introduction, give some specific reflections about the nature of prophecy. He sees the prophet as a man in whom the divine truth, which is like a 'seed which in itself is as dead as the seed of a plant without earth',[2] breaks forth. This might appear at first

[1] J. WELLHAUSEN, op. cit., p. 80.
[2] H. EWALD, *The Prophets of the Old Testament*, Eng. tr., London and Edinburgh, 1875, I, p. 3.

as an idealistic approach, but one is reminded more of Herder, in that the prophet is regarded as a mysterious manifestation of individuality. A prophet, however, cannot be understood simply in terms of himself. 'He has seen or heard something which does not concern him, or at least himself alone, and which allows him no peace.'[1] He emphasizes strongly that 'there can be no true prophet of Yahweh who has not first viewed the full majesty and holiness of Yahweh himself, and who has thereby become so completely filled with the true eternal life that it now lives on as a new life firmly established in him'.[2] Only on the basis of this encounter does the formulation of pure ideas, statements and propositions emerge. 'The great advantage of a vision over a pure proposition lies in the fact that it arises directly from real life, and so just as directly intervenes in it. . . . The true vision carries in itself the seed of active intervention into the needs of the present, both for the prophet in whose spirit it catches fire, as well as for the hearers who receive it. For this reason it is infinitely superior to ordinary speech.'[3] Here there is a clear rejection of both Rationalism, as well as of a pure philosophical Idealism. The prophet is a man touched by God, who is not only called to a new insight, but to a new life, and who also calls others into it.

Thus the prophet appears as a figure in whom something entirely new breaks forth for the first time. What then is the relationship of Moses to the prophets? Ewald deals only in general terms with this problem. He establishes that Old Testament prophecy appeared in a particular situation. 'The covenant with Yahweh . . . was a form and pattern of religion which even at the time when it originated, left still older and simpler forms of religion far behind, and surpassed all other religions. It was already an ascent to a pure spiritual religion; an upsurge of the human spirit to the purest divine thoughts and endeavours.'[4] However, this covenant (we could replace this term here by 'Moses') . . . was given in the earliest and most youthful period of antiquity, and therefore in a time when relatively few basic truths could be established. A multiplicity of further truths, relevant to the whole labyrinth of life, still needed to be revealed so that the prophetic activity also was quite indispensable.'[5] The ancient truth, given by Moses in the laws of the Pentateuch, became the proper basis for the prophets and aroused them to rise higher still in their knowledge. 'In the name of

[1] Ibid., p. 7. [2] Ibid., p. 26.
[3] Ibid., pp. 33 f. [4] Ibid., pp. 22 f.
[5] Ibid., p. 23.

Yahweh, and the ideas and traditions connected with it, there lay for them an unceasing magic.'

We can detect at this point a certain obscurity in Ewald's position. How are we to understand him? Does he mean that when Moses established the covenant in the name of Yahweh the whole depth of the knowledge of the divine was already given at that time, but was not fully grasped by the people? Are the prophets to some extent Moses' helpers, who assisted in the full unfolding of the knowledge which was already given then? Or is Ewald's opinion that the knowledge was still only fragmentary in Moses' time, and that the prophets, going beyond him, recognized more and more the full truth? Ewald gives no clear answer to this in his writing, which is more adulatory than precisely instructive.

The following period attempted to give the answer by way of a new historical picture of the development of the Old Testament faith. I cannot describe this development in detail, which was made possible by a number of careful studies on the part of many scholars. I must be content with describing one outstanding figure, who was able to set forth a major new synthesis so convincingly that he has left his stamp on a whole period of research. I would like to speak about a pupil of Ewald's, Julius Wellhausen and his work.

I would like here also to give some colour to the description, and to mention some personal details of the man whose name has become for many a shibboleth. Julius Wellhausen was born in Hameln in 1844 as the son of a minister, and studied oriental languages in Göttingen under Ewald. He became a lecturer in 1870, and in 1872 was called as professor ordinarius to the theological faculty in Greifswald. In the ten years spent in Greifswald he wrote his decisive studies on the literary criticism of the Old Testament. In 1882 he resigned from his professorship in the theological faculty. The letter to the ministerium, in which he tendered his resignation, is an impressive testimony to the integrity of this great man. He writes in this letter, 'I became a theologian because I was interested in the scientific treatment of the Bible. It has only slowly dawned upon me that a professor of theology has at the same time the task of preparing students for service in the Protestant Church, and that I am not adequate to perform this practical task. Since then my theological professorship has weighed heavily on my conscience.'[1] Thus Wellhausen retired on the grounds of conscience from

[1] A. JEPSEN, 'Wellhausen in Greifswald', *Festschrift zur 500-Jahrfeier der Universität Greifswald*, II, 1956, p. 54.

his theological professorship, and accepted the appointment of extraordinary professor for Semitic languages in Halle. In 1885 he was appointed ordinary professor for Semitic languages in Marburg, but was expressly forbidden to teach Old Testament because of his awesome reputation as a literary critic. In 1892 he moved to Göttingen, becoming a member of the philosophical faculty, to which Old Testament studies at that time belonged, and remained there until 1918. In his later years he wrote particularly on Arabic subjects, and then finally on the New Testament.

Wellhausen started his work with the criticism of the Pentateuch. His special achievement was that he set out a brilliant summary of the critical analysis of the Pentateuch which had been begun in the eighteenth century, and related this to a new presentation of the history of Israel. He was able to take up the earlier work of Vatke, who in 1835 had published a very abstruse volume on Old Testament theology, written in Hegelian thought-forms, and the work of Reuss and Graf.

Wellhausen himself tells how he arrived at his new point of view. At the commencement of his studies he dealt with the personalities of the historical books of the Old Testament, with Saul and David, and then with the prophetic figures of Amos and Isaiah. He became very dissatisfied with this, and he mentions that, 'It was as if I were beginning with the roof instead of the foundation.'[1] Thereupon he turned his attention to the foundation and studied the Pentateuch, working through Exodus, Leviticus and Numbers with passionate care. 'But in vain I waited for the light which these should have thrown on the historical and prophetic books. On the contrary the law spoiled for me the enjoyment of these writings, and instead of making them more familiar to me, it intruded into them, like a ghost which makes a noise, but is not seen, and really effects nothing. . . . I vaguely felt a great gulf between two different worlds.'[2] Then on an occasional visit to Göttingen in 1867, to the house of Albrecht Ritschl, the systematic theologian, he became acquainted with the thesis of Graf, who placed the law after the prophets. Wellhausen said, 'Almost without knowing the reasons for his hypothesis I was won over to it.'[3]

Thus Wellhausen developed his great thesis under the key sentence: 'The law is later than the prophets.' After a detailed critical analysis in *Die Composition des Hexateuchs*, he presented the results in 1878 in a book

---

[1] J. WELLHAUSEN, *Prolegomena zur Geschichte Israels*, Berlin, 1883; Eng. trans., Edinburgh, 1885, *Prolegomena to the History of Israel*, p. 3.
[2] Ibid., p. 3.   [3] Ibid.

entitled *Geschichte Israels I*, which in later editions was called *Prolegomena zur Geschichte Israels*. The source which, in the books of Moses from Exodus to Numbers, reports the great promulgation of the law, the setting up of the tabernacle, the institution of the cult and the investiture of the priests, is a document of the post-exilic period, and has only subsequently been transposed into the narrative of the early history of Israel. It now appears in this context as the account of how the theocracy was first established. In reality the beginning of the history of Israel was characterized by free religious instruction by priests and prophets, delivered orally. In it both custom and tradition were understood as the will of God. At that time there was no '*torah* existing independently as a complete system, which was available to everybody'. Such instruction 'only existed in individual sayings, which gradually constituted a fixed tradition'. In such a situation the great prophets also emerged. 'Their significance is based on the individual. . . . Great men always stand alone, quite by themselves.'[1] The inspiration of individuals is the decisive factor here. They live in the storms of world history. 'They speak in the power of the spirit, which judges all things, but is itself judged by no one. Where do they claim support on any other authority than the evidence? Where do they build on any other foundation than that of their own certainty? . . . Their creed is not written in any book. It would be barbarous to disfigure the shape of such a phenomenon with the law.'[2]

Only towards the end of the period of the monarchy does the position change with the law book of Josiah, referred to in 2 Kings xxii, and which Wellhausen identified with the kernel of Deuteronomy on the basis of the earlier hypothesis of de Wette. Here the fact of a book begins to assume importance. 'With the appearance of the law liberty was at an end. . . . There now existed a completely objective authority; that meant the death of prophecy.'[3] With this there took place a metamorphosis of the theocracy from an idea into an institution.

Wellhausen's results brought an entirely new position in regard to our problem of the law and the prophets. For centuries both the Jewish and Christian traditions had regarded Moses as the great mediator and lawgiver of Israel, who had given to his people in God's name its sacred order of life, in which all the ensuing generations, the prophets included, had lived. Now this whole great order and institution was removed from its position of primacy. Thus also the prophets with their preach-

[1] Ibid., p. 398.   [2] Ibid.. pp. 398 f.
[3] Ibid., p. 402

ing came to stand in a new light. They were no longer regarded as followers and as interpreters of an already existent law, but they themselves were the originating figures.

In his book *Israelitische und Jüdische Geschichte*, which appeared in 1894, Wellhausen presented his case with even greater precision. In this it becomes clear that Moses is in no way completely eliminated. He remains the great man of God, who led Israel out of Egypt into the region of Kadesh. At that time a decisive and formative event must have taken place. 'The prophets accentuated the uniqueness of Israel, but they did not create it. It was presupposed by them.'[1] The foundation of Israel is the belief that 'Yahweh is the God of Israel, and Israel is the people of Yahweh'. The achievement of Moses was to have made this belief the basis of Israel. Through his authority he became the great lawgiver of his people, so that in a certain sense he created a tradition of law among them. God was always the God of law and of righteousness, and this tradition continued to be vitally maintained by the priests. Nevertheless 'the priestly *torah* was a completely non-political and pre-political institution. It existed before the state and was one of its invisible foundations.'[2] If we ask how ultimately this relationship between Yahweh and Israel came about, then Wellhausen answers, 'This relationship was hereditary and natural; it was indissoluble and was not based on the stipulations of a contract.'[3]

What then is the achievement of the prophets? According to Wellhausen, they introduced a universal view of history into the faith of Israel. 'Events did not take them by surprise, so that they were thrown into hopeless despair; they solved in advance the fearful problem which history posed. They adopted the idea of the world, which destroyed the religions of the nations, into their religion, into the nature of Yawheh. . . . The nations are the agents, Israel is the hero, and Yahweh is the poet of the tragedy. . . . Events are simply the occasion which sets free the progress of morality and of the knowledge of God.'[4] In this regard Wellhausen can sometimes use the concept of law in quite a positive way. The prophets 'place the idea of the covenant, though not its name, at the centre of their faith, and with it the corresponding concept of law'. They make it the foundation of their religion, and, as a consequence, demand a social righteousness.

The statutory law, on the other hand, only emerges later. The

[1] J. WELLHAUSEN, *Israelitische und Jüdische Geschichte* (1 Aufl.), Berlin, 1894, p. 13.
[2] Ibid., p. 16.   [3] Ibid., p. 68.
[4] Ibid., p. 76.

chapter of Wellhausen's book which deals with Ezra is explicitly
entitled 'The Law'.

We must examine now the importance of Wellhausen's thesis for
our study of the law and the prophets. Wellhausen wanted to be a
historian, and not a theologian. Nevertheless he believed that through
his historical studies he would contribute to the knowledge of God. A
sentence from a letter to Dillmann shows this very clearly. He writes,
'If I were to express myself plainly, I would say that Ewald's *Metra
Carminum Arabicorum* has done more for the rebirth of the Church
than all that Pfleiderer and Holtzmann have written about the direct
relationship of science and religion. Science is above everything else a
matter of self-denial.'[1] Thus we do not find in his work any systematic
reflections about the relationship between law and prophecy. In fact we
have seen that his use of the term 'law' was inconsistent. If we concern
ourselves with what he especially terms 'law', and which he connects
with the Priestly Document and with Ezra, then it is clear that he could
no longer see the two entities, law and prophecy, as bound in an inner
unity, as earlier scholarship had done. He saw them in a historical
sequence. Prophecy was a breaking through of truth, whereas in the
law a particular hardening of this truth took place. 'Moses', when dis-
sociated from such a law encrusted in statutes, represented the beginning
of a genuine simplicity which preceded both. Wellhausen's thought
cannot be forced into a system, and he himself guarded against doing
so. He never worked out a theological concept of law. For him revelation took place in the course of history, and reached its climax in the
gospel. Contrary to the earlier editions of his *Israelitische und Jüdische
Geschichte*, in the later editions Wellhausen deliberately placed the chapter
bearing the heading 'the Gospel' at the end. He introduced the age of the
gospel with the opening words, 'A sower went out to sow his seed. The
seed was the Word, and the soil was Time.'[2] In regard to its content he
outlines the goal to which the gospel leads: 'The religion of the gospel is
individualism, the freedom of the children of God. Jesus did not found
the Church; he passed sentence upon the Jewish theocracy. The representatives of the law understood it, but they were, naturally, not con-

---

[1] E. BARNIKOL, 'Wellhausens Briefe aus seiner Greifswalder Zeit (1872–9) an
den anderen Heinrich-Ewald-Schüler Dillmann', *Wissenschaftliche Zeitschrift
Halle-Wittenberg*. Gesellschafts-sprachwissenschaftliche Reihe VI/5, 1957, pp.
701–12; also in *Gottes ist der Orient*. Festschrift for O. Eissfeldt on his seventieth
birthday, Halle, 1959, pp. 28–39, here p. 32.

[2] J. WELLHAUSEN, *Israelitische und Jüdische Geschichte*, p. 308.

tent with it. They rejected the gospel and canonized the book of Esther.'[1] Again the key-word 'law' reappears. Law is here seen as the written code, which embodied in the post-exilic age the inheritance of the prophetic era. Through Christ this inheritance received its full freedom.

Wellhausen's critical work made possible quite new perspectives in Old Testament study. Above all prophecy was laid open to examination as a quite independent phenomenon. The stimulus of Herder and Ewald could now become effective in a new way. I would like to illustrate this from the work of two scholars who wrote particularly able books on the prophets.

The first is Bernhard Duhm, who was born in 1847 in East Frisia. In 1871 he became tutor in Göttingen, a lecturer in 1873 and professor extraordinary in 1877. In 1888 he became ordinary professor in Basel, and died there in 1928, over eighty years old, as the victim of a tragic motor accident. Duhm dealt twice with the prophets in a comprehensive way. In 1875, before Wellhausen's *Geschichte Israels I* (*Prolegomena*) had appeared, he published his *Theologie der Propheten*. The fuller title of this book describes it as 'a Basis for the Inner History of Development of the Israelite Religion', which already in some regard anticipates Wellhausen's view. In fact Duhm goes further, and shows a striking connection with what Wellhausen said about Moses. 'In the formula: Israel is the people of Yahweh, and Yahweh is the God of Israel the whole content of the prophetic religion is completely expressed.'[2] Even more influential was the popular presentation which appeared in 1916 under the title *Israels Propheten*. At the beginning of this book there is a brief treatment of Moses. His achievement was to have led Israel out of Egypt. He cannot, therefore, be regarded as the lawgiver of Israel. The Decalogue in Exodus xx was placed by Duhm in a much later age. 'It reflects the transition from a cultic to an ethical religion, which was, as far as we know, accomplished by the prophets of the eighth century.'[3] These prophets were the really creative figures of Israel. They were men with a new and powerful experience, who, in prophetic visions, foretold the coming world catastrophe'. 'They set the relationship between God and people on a purely moral basis'.[4] In doing so, however, they in no way intended to replace religion with mere morality. 'Such men who have visions and auditions, and therefore stand in a real relationship to the living God, could never arrive

---

[1] Ibid., p. 321.   [2] B. DUHM, *Theologie der Propheten*, Bonn, 1875, p. 96.
[3] B. DUHM, *Israels Propheten*, Tübingen, 1916, p. 39.   [4] Ibid., p. 140.

at such a thought.'[1] They were reformers preparing for the 'religion of the soul'. They strove to free religion from sensuousness, and to lift it up to the level of moral communion between free personalities'.

Later on the prophetic movement died out. After the exile, through Ezra and Nehemiah, Israel became the people of the *torah*, under obligation to a code of laws. 'The lawgiver is the antithesis of the prophet. Judaism, which no longer understood the prophets, nor the earlier period as a whole, chose for itself the lawgiver. . . . The people of Yahweh became the people of the *torah*.'[2] Even more decisively than with Wellhausen the great spiritual individual personalities of the prophets, with their rich experience and ethical concern, are set in opposition to the law and lawgivers which followed them. Moses, who is counted among the older prophets, is completely overshadowed. In the emphasis upon the personal experiences and individuality of the prophets we can discern the influence of Herder, whilst the stress upon ethical spirituality betrays the inheritance of Idealism. Even here, however, we cannot speak of a theologically conceived concept of law. Law is for Duhm something statutory, institutional, and external, whilst for him the prophets were men of freedom, spirituality, and a personal individualism in direct communion with God.

It is quite easy to understand that on this basis the religious psychological aspect of the prophetic experience took on a new interest. Influenced by Wundt's *Völkerpsychologie*, Gustav Hölscher, whom I should like to mention as the second of the scholars who devoted their attention to the prophets, published a book entitled *Die Profeten. Untersuchungen zur Religionsgeschichte Israels* in 1914.[3] He was born in 1877, and, like Duhm, came from East Frisia. He qualified as a lecturer in Halle in 1905, became an extraordinary professor there in 1915, and after 1920 he taught as a professor in Giessen, Marburg, Bonn and Heidelberg, where he died in 1955. In the above mentioned book Hölscher examined particularly the psychological phenomena of the prophetic experience: exalted ecstasy, the ecstatic cult dance, apathic ecstasy, compulsive movements and actions, speaking in tongues, hallucinations, hypnotic visions, amnesia, trance, clairvoyance and other phenomena. He particularly dealt with ecstasy and visions, and examined the individual parts of the ecstatic experience. Hölscher believed that this ecstatic aspect of the prophets of Israel derived from

[1] Ibid., p. 140.   [2] Ibid., p. 391.
[3] G. HÖLSCHER, *Die Profeten. Untersuchung zur Religionsgeschichte Israels*, Leipzig, 1914.

Canaan. Besides this a second source is found in the early mantics, the seers and diviners to which analogies are to be found in early Arabia, where we have evidence of night-visions, incantations and divination. In early Arabia these phenomena appear to have been connected with the activity of priests. According to Hölscher Moses was the priest of the sanctuary at the oasis of Kadesh, where Israel stayed for a period during the desert wandering, and thus he belonged to this area. The connection of Moses with the exodus from Egypt was thought by Hölscher to be a secondary development. Moses belonged to the tribe of Levi in the vicinity of Kadesh, where, according to tradition, he was the founder of the cult of Yahweh. These priestly seers mainly employed the technique of obtaining oracles through the casting of lots, and *torah* means primarily the casting of such sacred lots. In these two originally separate phenomena of ecstatic and mantic prophecy are to be found the two roots of later prophecy, which admittedly developed into something of incomparably greater value. It led to the knowledge of 'the exalted and moral God of heaven and earth. Prophecy did not originate this new and higher view, but its inspired enthusiasm gave the highest and most compelling expression to a purified doctrine of God.'[1] Hölscher himself says that in this 'lies the beginning of personal religion', in which laymen, without any priestly mediation, could enter into direct relationship with the deity. They refined 'the cultic religion into a religion of morality, and the religion of nature into a religion of history'.[2]

In his book on the prophets Hölscher does not express any positive opinion concerning the law. He does, however, make clear how he regarded the subsequent development in his evaluation of the reconstruction programme at the end of the book of Ezekiel. 'The ethical spiritualizing of religion, by which the older prophecy had forced the cultic element into the background, now once again took a step backwards.'[3]

There are a number of further studies which ought to be mentioned here, which particularly dealt with the religious psychological aspect of prophecy. These include the attempt by Allwohn to interpret psychoanalytically the sign of the marriage of the prophet Hosea,[4] and the pathological study by Karl Jaspers on Ezekiel, in which he sought to

[1] Ibid., pp. 185 f.   [2] Ibid., pp. 187 f.
[3] Ibid., p. 314.
[4] A. ALLWOHN, 'Die Ehe des Propheten Hosea in psychoanalytischer Beleuchtung', *BZAW* 44, Giessen, 1926.

diagnose schizophrenia on medical grounds.[1] These studies have been
of value in bringing to light the strangeness of many features of the
prophets, which a rationalistic interpretation of them overlooked. They
have, however, more than once overstepped the limits of the evidence
in seeking to understand the unusual features. The phenomenon of
prophecy cannot be illuminated by the psychology of religion in its
most unique feature; the message which it brought.

Wellhausen's major discovery can be summarized as an assertion that
the law is later than the prophets. He established this thesis on the basis
ot the literary criticism of the Pentateuch, and asserted in detail that the
Priestly Document, as well as Deuteronomy, are both later than the
prophets. When this is put round the other way it means that the
prophets do not presuppose the cultic laws of the Priestly Document.
Since Wellhausen this thesis has been modified in detail, and has been
stated with greater precision. It has also become clear, however, that
the traditio-historical question of the origin and age of the material
of the Priestly Document is still left unanswered. Nevertheless within
the framework of literary critical studies, this thesis remains the great
and valid achievement of Wellhausen.

It can now be seen, however, that this thesis leaves open an important
question. Even after the subtraction from the Pentateuch of the Priestly
Document, as Wellhausen proposed, and of Deuteronomy, as de Wette
had previously proposed, there still remains an element of law, which
is rooted in the older sources. How is this law to be evaluated? Wellhausen's thesis that the law is later than the prophets shows the limita-
tions which such catch-phrases usually have. They do not cover all the
facts. This unsolved problem can be clearly seen in the uncertainty of
the conclusions about the figure of Moses, who received far more careful treatment from Wellhausen than from many who came after him.
How far do the prophets stand in an older tradition which may be
summed up by the name of Moses? How far does Moses, or at least
the law which came to bear his name at a very early period, precede
the very independent figures of the prophets? This problem of the older
law in Israel now calls for further examination, and under it the question
of the relationship between the law and the prophets appears in a new
light.

[1] KARL JASPERS, 'Der Prophet Ezechiel. Eine pathographische Studie', *Festschrift K. Schneider*, 1947, pp. 1–9.

III. Law and Covenant

WE must now examine the question of the oldest divine commandments to Israel. Wellhausen's penetrating criticism showed that the narrative of the Priestly Document, with its account of the giving of the law was formulated at a comparatively late period. It is valuable first of all then to consider how the traditional picture of the giving of the law by Moses appears once Wellhausen's literary criticism has been applied. We must look again at the older sources of the Yahwist and Elohist.

Exodus xix tells how the people of Israel came to the mount of God in the desert after the exodus from Egypt. There Moses received from God instructions how the people were to prepare themselves for an encounter with Yahweh. On the third day there was thunder and lightning, and Mount Sinai was wrapped in smoke from the fire in which Yahweh descended upon it. The people stood at the foot of the mountain, and received from God the ten commandments, which are described in Exodus xx. 1–17. In terror the people asked Moses to speak with God on their behalf, because they were unable to stand before his presence. Moses therefore went up into the cloud and received a great number of further commandments described in Exodus xx. 22–xxiii. 33. Exodus xxiv then relates how Moses afterwards wrote down the commandments in a book and read them aloud during the covenant ceremony at the foot of the mountain. This collection is therefore called the Book of the Covenant. Exodus xxiv. 7 f. expressly says: 'Then he took the book of the covenant, and read it in the hearing of the people; and they said, "All that Yahweh has spoken we will do, and we will be obedient". And Moses took the blood and threw it upon the people and said, "Behold the blood of the covenant which Yahweh has made with you in accordance with all these words".' After the account of a visit of a delegation from the people upon the mountain where they ate a covenant meal in the presence of the glory of Yahweh, Moses is summoned once again to ascend the mountain in order to receive the stone tablets of the law. According to the older account in Exodus xxxii–xxxiv, which originally immediately followed chapter xxiv, Moses descended again after forty days, and found the people committing a great sin with the golden calf. Moses made expiation for this transgression by severely punishing the people, but Yahweh sent the people away from his mountain. Exodus xxxiv then tells of a second giving of commandments, and the handing over of new tablets, since Moses had broken the original ones when he saw the people's sin after he had come down from the mountain. The report of the departure from the mountain, which is found in Numbers x. 29 ff. must have followed at this point in the oldest sources. The entire intervening material from Exodus xxxv–Numbers x is from the Priestly Document.

Thus after the amputation of the material of the Priestly Document only the two law collections of the Decalogue and the Book of the Covenant, plus the statutes found in Exodus xxxiv, are left for the older tradition. These law collections now demand our special attention. Is something of the oldest legal tradition to be found here, so that we have in it a law of Israel which antedates the prophets?

It is easy to understand that the Decalogue has always been regarded with special interest among these older collections of law, and the Christian Church has always attached particular importance to it as a part of its catechetical teaching. The fact that the Decalogue is repeated in Deuteronomy v shows that it must also have had a special significance for ancient Israel as well.

There is, however, in dealing with the Decalogue a peculiar additional difficulty, which was already apparent to Goethe. In 1773 he wrote a treatise under the title *Two Important Biblical Questions Thus Far Unexamined and Now for the First Time Thoroughly Answered by a Country Parson in Swabia*.[1] In it he considered first of all the question: what was written on the tablets of the covenant? He gave as an answer: not the ten commandments, the first part of our catechism. He establishes first that, according to Exodus xxxii, the first tablets were broken by Moses on his descent from the mountain. Then, according to Exodus xxxiv, when Moses was again with God on the mountain, he was given several additional commandments, and was told, 'Write these words down, for in accordance with these words I have made a covenant with you and with Israel. . . . And he wrote upon the tablets the words of the covenant, the ten words'.[2] Therefore the tablets that were preserved contained the commandments of Exodus xxxiv, which regulate special features of the Old Testament cult, and which in no way shows the

---

[1] J. W. GOETHE, *Zwo wichtige, bisher unerörterte biblische Fragen zum erstenmal gründlich beantwortet von einem Landgeistlichen in Schwaben* (Weimarer Ausgabe 37, pp. 177–90; Jubilee edition 36, pp. 95–105).

[2] Exod. xxxiv. 27, 28b. RSV footnote reading.

broad ethical concern of the Decalogue of the catechism. Goethe concluded that the original decalogue of Israel did not yet have the spiritual breadth of the Decalogue of Exodus xx. 'I regard the Jewish people as a wild unfruitful stock, which stood in a circle of wild unfruitful trees upon which the eternal gardener has grafted the noble scion Jesus Christ. . . . The history and doctrine of this people from their first origins to their engrafting is completely particular. . . . Starting with the engrafting the entire situation changes. Doctrine and history become universal.'

Goethe betrays the interests of his own age in explaining the differences between the two decalogues by the categories of 'particular' and 'universal'. In the history of subsequent critical research the question of assigning these passages to the various sources was bound up with this evaluation, which is constantly re-echoed. The more ancient decalogue of Exodus xxxiv was attributed to the older source of the so-called Yahwist, whilst that of Exodus xx was attributed to the Elohist.

Only gradually did the realization emerge that the Decalogue of Exodus xx is a document *sui generis*, which cannot simply be ascribed to a narrative stratum, even though it now appears to be embedded in one. With the recognition of the distinctive nature of the classical Decalogue, however, there arose a much more critical evaluation of Exodus xxxiv. Do we really find a decalogue here? The attempt to isolate ten commandments has never been really successful and convincing. Nonetheless the thesis of a Yahwistic decalogue still haunts scholarship. In my opinion we can set it aside here with a good conscience, and concentrate entirely upon the Decalogue of Exodus xx (= Deut. v), which we no longer ought to describe as the Elohistic Decalogue.

The study of the Decalogue, for which there is a considerable literature,[1] poses first of all the question whether it is of Mosaic, or post-Mosaic origin. This is related to the further question of whether the Decalogue of Exodus xx is in its original form, or whether it has undergone expansion. The latter question is necessitated by a comparison of of the version of Exodus xx with that of Deuternomy v, where many details, especially in the motivation of the sabbath commandment, show noticeable differences. In Exodus xx the sabbath commandment

---

[1] Cf. L. KÖHLER, *ThR* (NF) 1, 1929, pp. 161–84; H. H. ROWLEY, 'Moses and the Decalogue', *BJRL* 34, 1951, pp. 81–118, reprinted in *Men of God*, London, 1963, pp. 1–36; J. J. Stamm, *ThR* (NF) 27, 1961, pp. 189–239; 281–305.

is motivated on cosmological grounds by a reference to the six days of creation, followed by God's day of rest, whilst Deuteronomy v points to the saving act of Israel's liberation from the house of bondage in Egypt. Thus the slave also must be considered, and allowed to rest on this day. Today it is generally accepted that there was an original Decalogue, which contained the ten commandments in a quite terse form. H. Graf Reventlow, in his recent work *Gebot und Predigt im Dekalog*,[1] reckons on a lengthy period of preaching activity, through which the Decalogue constantly received expansions.

Opinions diverge sharply over the question of the Mosaic origin of the Decalogue. After the Mosaic authorship of the whole Pentateuchal law could no longer be maintained, conservative scholarship fought passionately to maintain that at least in the Decalogue we have an authentic formulation of the teaching of Moses. A good example is Paul Volz's book *Mose und sein Werk*,[2] where the entire understanding of Moses is developed from the Decalogue. One section bears the title 'The Decalogue as the Statute and Programme of Moses'. The personal achievement of Moses is seen behind this programme of the Decalogue. Following the analogy of history, Volz claims, 'It has been shown again and again that some mighty genius stands at the beginning of powerful and historically significant movements, a genius who transcends his own time, whose endowments run way ahead of the centuries, requiring centuries for their appropriation.'[3] Hence it is probable that 'a genius of the first order' stands at the beginning of Old Testament religion. Thus Moses can be known through the Decalogue.

The views of the critical school are in sharp contrast with these conservative opinions. According to Wellhausen the so-called Yahwistic decalogue, because of the greater antiquity of its content, is older than the Elohistic Decalogue, which, in contrast, marks an extremely significant advance, comparable to the advance of Amos over his contemporaries.[4] We can already see here that such evaluations are made on the basis of considerations regarding the general progress of spirituality. The lofty morality of the prophets is found in the Decalogue, which is then dated according to the general pattern of development.

It is not to be denied that both the conservative as well as the more

---

[1] GÜTERSLOH, 1962.

[2] P. VOLZ, *Mose und sein Werk* (2. Aufl.), Tübingen, 1932.

[3] Ibid., p. 12.

[4] Cf. R. SMEND, *Das Mosebild von Heinrich Ewald bis Martin Noth*, Tübingen, 1959, p. 9.

Law and Covenant

35

critical scholars make their judgments from very closely related positions, in spite of the differences in their results. For both groups particular premises regarding the history of spiritual development have shaped their point of view. For Volz it is the assumption that great spiritual movements originate with a genius; he then proves the spirituality of this genius from the individual commandments. The critical school begins with the idea that the Old Testament faith develops into ethical religion, and in this context values the Decalogue as a document marking a certain stage of spiritual development.

It has become increasingly plain, however, that these general conclusions, based on ideas of spiritual development, offer no real advance. New impulses, and new methods of examining the text, were necessary for real progress, and these have in fact developed subsequently.

We must consider two new possibilities of research, which have revitalized the stagnant discussion about ancient Israelite law. The first is a new method of examining the text, namely the form-critical approach, with its new methodology. The second is the increase in our material knowledge from previously unknown sources.

For the first point we may start with an investigation of the Decalogue published in 1927 by the unusually productive and stimulating Old Testament scholar in Oslo, Sigmund Mowinckel (born 1884). In this study, *Le Décalogue*, Mowinckel on the one hand pays his respects to the then current approach by starting from the source division of the two decalogues, and deriving Exodus xx from the disciples of Isaiah. That which really pointed the way forward, however, was something else. Mowinckel sought to determine the place where the Decalogue had its roots in real life. He examined the narratives of the exodus and Sinai events and concluded, 'The accounts of J and E are nothing other than a reproduction of a New Year Festival, the Enthronement and Covenant-renewal Festival, which was celebrated in Jerusalem, now translated into the language of historical myth.'[1] In this festival is to be found the setting of the Decalogue. He compared with it the twelve-fold curse formula of Deuteronomy xxvii. 14–26, and Psalms l and lxxxi, where such a use of the Decalogue in worship can be recognized. Similarly Psalms xv and xxiv, which were part of a Jerusalem festival liturgy, show that attendance at the great festivals was bound by cultic regulations, and that the temple worshipper was questioned concerning his observance of them.

In this approach Mowinckel is a disciple of Hermann Gunkel, who

[1] S. Mowinckel, *Le Décalogue*, Paris, 1927, p. 129.

had made use of an analagous approach in his classic studies on Genesis
and on the Psalms. Gunkel had wanted to get behind the literary
documents, in which the previous era of scholarship had been ex-
clusively interested, to the oral source of the separate units, and had
sought to understand their growth from these origins. The interest in
particular forms and stereotyped patterns was closely connected with
this. Thus the form-critical approach was born. By means of this
approach the different passages came to stand in a completely new
light. We may even claim that in this way scholarship freed itself from
its idealistic tendency, which was solely interested in the intellectual
content of the material. The new approach was not only interested in
the development of particular ideas, isolated from their concrete
embodiment in life, but also in the entire activity and situation which
lay behind the individual literary units. Thus it has become necessary
to examine the *Sitz im Leben*, the 'setting in life' of the material. The
individual passages are seen as rooted in a particular life situation, which
gives rise to a particular form of expression. Behind the lamentations
of the people in the Psalms there is seen the concrete activity of a day
of penitence, and of the liturgy for days of fasting. Similarly behind the
individual aetiological sagas of Genesis we can recognize attempts to
explain certain national and geographical phenomena.

It was Mowinckel's accomplishment to have used this approach in
the study of the Decalogue. He sought to discover the life situation in
which this, and comparable related texts, originated. By this approach
certain formal characteristics came unexpectedly into a new light.
Observations which had already been made previously now received
a new significance in a larger context.

Why, for example, are there exactly ten commandments? The conservative Old Testament scholar Hengstenberg was still able to say,
'The number ten is the symbol of what is perfect and complete in
itself.'[1] Thus even the number ten is the expression of an idea. Ewald
had already established from the *pempasasthai* mentioned in the
Odyssey iv. 412, and in Plutarch's *Isis and Osiris* lvi, that here we see the
very simplest manner of counting in terms of the fingers of both hands.[2]
When Gunkel re-examined this observation in terms of a particular
Sitz im Leben, and said, 'The ten commandments were put together to
be learned by heart, arranged according to the ten fingers of our

[1] E. W. Hengstenberg, *Dissertations on the Genuineness of the Pentateuch*, Eng.
trans., Edinburgh, 1847, II, p. 320.
[2] H. Ewald, *The History of Israel*, Eng. trans., London, 1867, Vol. I, pp. 582 f.

hands',[1] then the practical application of this ten-word pattern in Israel's worship became clearly recognizable. The number ten was arrived at, not for the sake of some high idea, but for the sake of the quite practical necessity of better retention. The Decalogue was taken out of the setting of some high idea, and was understood simply as a collection of ten injunctions put together for practical catechetical reasons. The individual injunctions could then have existed even before their collection into a series of ten.

We must now set alongside this possibility of a new method of approach a second factor. This is the great enrichment of our knowledge concerning Israel's environment in the Ancient Near East, which archaeological excavations have brought about in increasing measure. As regards law the most famous discovery was that of the great law code of Hammurabi ,which is now in the Louvre, and which was found in 1901–2 in the Elamite capital of Susa. Subsequently other ancient law codes have appeared, Assyrian, Hittite and Sumerian.[2] From all of these it has been possible to infer an extensive Ancient Near Eastern legal system, which transcended national boundaries.

Attention was focused very quickly on the close relationship of this legal material to particular Old Testament laws. Above all the Book of the Covenant proved to be a very rewarding object of comparison. In addition to an examination of contents, in which prominent jurists participated, the form-critical approach was employed. Thus A. Jepsen published in 1927 a study entitled *Untersuchungen zum Bundesbuch,*[3] in which he sought to analyse the Book of the Covenant form-critically. He claimed to have found four sources in it; (1) The Hebrew *mishpatim* in Exodus xxi. 1 ff., which, on account of their form and content, showed the closest contacts with Ancient Near Eastern law. Jepsen derived these from the Hebrews, whom he identified with the Habiru of the Amarna letters. (2) the Israelite *mishpatim*, which are statutes of the type found in Exodus xxi. 12, 'whoever strikes a man so that he dies shall be put to death'. Behind these he sees laws established in Israel by God. (3) Religious and moral prohibitions such as Exodus xxii. 18 (Heb. 17): 'You shall not permit a sorceress to live', and finally (4) the cultic stipulations of the Book of the Covenant, in which the first opposition of Israel to Canaanite practice can be recognized.

---

[1] H. GUNKEL, 'Die Israelitische Literatur', *Die Kultur der Gegenwart I: 7,* Stuttgart, 1906, p. 75.

[2] *ANET,* pp. 159–222.

[3] A. JEPSEN, *Untersuchungen zum Bundesbuch (BWANT* III: 5), Stuttgart, 1927.

Jepsen's study was written under the influence of Albrecht Alt, who himself published in 1934 a work entitled *die Ursprünge des Israelitischen Rechts*, which was a great achievement of simplicity and comprehensiveness. In its concise clarity this work is in some ways reminiscent of Wellhausen's achievement. It has brought new life to the study of the ancient laws of the Old Testament in a very special way. Contemporary scholarship is still very much concerned with this monograph, whether by agreement with it, or in opposition to it. Primarily intended as a strict form-critical and legal-historical study, this work has also begun to open the way to an entirely new theological investigation concerning the significance of the law in the Old Testament. Thus it is very appropriate that we should examine its major thesis more closely.

Alt's work centres on the Book of the Covenant and draws on other legal formulations only for further clarification. In the Book of the Covenant he concludes that two streams of law of very different character and origin have come together. On the one hand we have the so-called casuistic laws, which Jepsen had designated as Hebrew *mishpatim*. This type of law, which is found in Exodus xxi. 1–xxii. 17 (Heb. 16) (with a few interruptions), is called causistic because here specific legal cases are defined, from which further subordinate cases are differentiated. For each case the appropriate judical action is stipulated. Thus, for instance, Exodus xxi. 18 f.: 'When men quarrel and one strikes the other with a stone or with his fist and the man does not die but keeps his bed, then if the man rises again and walks abroad with his staff, he that struck him shall be clear; only he shall pay for the loss of his time, and shall have him thoroughly healed.' Here a law case is described, using a formulation in the third person, with very detailed and exact stipulations, as close examination shows. The major circumstance is introduced by the Hebrew particle *ki* (= if), which is clearly differentiated from the subordinate circumstance introduced by the Hebrew *'im* (= if). In this case it is quite clear that the second possible subordinate circumstance would consist in the death of the man who had been struck. The stipulation of the appropriate punishment then follows. It is a very developed legal style, in which a law case is objectively described and so carefully defined by a series of brief and precise conditional clauses that the situation becomes perfectly clear. Then the appropriate punishment is clearly formulated. In Exodus xxi. 1 ff. we have a book of casuistic statutes, the beginning of which is preserved completely intact. The heading is given in Exodus xxi. 1, which designates this kind of statute as *mishpatim*. Further along we find interspersed instances of other juristic formulations, which may be clearly distinguished on form-critical grounds. At Exodus xxii. 17 (Heb. 16) the collection is suddenly broken off, and it seems that a part of the original continuation is to be found in Deuteronomy xxii.

The question of where such laws originated and were applied, in other words where they had their *Sitz im Leben*, may be answered by the assertion that they belonged to the normal court procedure which took place at the city gate. Ruth iv. 1 ff. beautifully describes how this court was summoned, and how it worked. In this case the matter dealt with was a question of establishing a right of redemption, or of first purchase. 'And Boaz went up to the gate and sat down there; and behold, the next of kin, of whom Boaz had spoken, came by. So Boaz said, "Turn aside, friend; sit down here", and he turned aside and sat down. And he took ten men of the elders of the city, and said, "Sit down here", so they sat down. Then he said to the next of kin, "Naomi, who has come back from the country of Moab, is selling the parcel of land which belonged to our kinsman Elimelech. So I thought I would tell you of it, and say, buy it in the presence of those sitting here, and in the presence of the elders of my people" . . .' Thus the case is discussed and clarified publicly in the circle of the respected elders of the city. This feature of Hebrew justice was very clearly described by Ludwig Köhler in a famous rectoral address given at Zürich in 1931.[1]

If we ask further concerning the origins of such law, we find that precisely this kind of law has rich parallels in the Ancient Near Eastern legal codes. The parallelism extends not only to the formal structure, but also to the content. Thus a case corresponding to the one cited from the Book of the Covenant is to be found in section 206 of Hammurabi's code: 'If a seignior has struck another seignior in a brawl and has inflicted an injury on him, that seignior shall swear, "I did not strike him deliberately"; and he shall also pay for the physician.'[2] The connection with the Ancient Near Eastern juristic culture was probably mediated by the Canaanites. Israel must have learnt this law from them in the time between the conquest and the formation of the state. It is no accident that in it specifically Israelite characteristics are very much in the background. Alt considered that it could have been handed down by the so-called 'minor judges' (Judges x. 1–5 and xii. 8–15).

For our present purpose the second type of legal material is more significant, which Alt summarized under the name 'apodictic law', although on many points he oversimplifies in his classification. In the

[1] Eng. trans., in L. Köhler, *Hebrew Man*, London, 1956.   [2] *ANET*, p. 153.

Book of the Covenant several types of law are to be clearly distinguished from the casuistic laws on account of their quite different formulation. It is best not to designate the *lex talionis*, the famous, 'eye for eye, tooth, for tooth, hand for hand, foot for foot . . .' (Exod. xxi. 23–25), as apodictic law, since, although it can clearly be distinguished from the casuistic law, it has its counterpart in Hammurabi's code. On the other hand another group of statutes may be recognized by their peculiar rhythm: 'Whoever strikes a man so that he dies, shall be put to death' (Exod. xxi. 12). The five-beat rhythm which characterizes this verse, reappears in the same form several verses later: 'Whoever strikes his father or his mother shall be put to death. Whoever steals a man . . . shall be put to death. Whoever curses his father or his mother shall be put to death' (Exod. xxi. 15–17).[1] The man's action is described by a participial clause, to which eventually the result of this action was added, and then the punishment is expressed by a verb strengthened with an infinitive absolute. These laws speak very forcefully, with no regard for ifs and buts, and throughout they recognize only the death penalty, in a very stereotyped way. The similarity of their formulation shows that they were put together in a series so that their recital would strengthen the note of severity which properly belongs to these terse laws. In our present text, however, the series is broken up. Parts of it are to be found scattered in the Book of the Covenant and the Holiness Code.

Alt places beside these laws the distinctive curse dodecalogue of Deuteronomy xxvii. 15–26. Twelve sayings, which must originally all have had the same four-beat metre, are here put side by side and are all introduced by the Hebrew ''*arur*' (= cursed). 'Cursed be the man who makes a graven image . . . Cursed be he who dishonours his father or his mother . . . Cursed be he who removes his neighbour's landmark . . .' Beside the series of capital crimes, we have a series of crimes which are cursed, though in particular instances they overlap. Since this series is partly concerned with secret crimes, we may understand that the execution of the punishment is put in Yahweh's hand by the curse formula, since he sees what is hidden. There is finally in Leviticus xviii a list of offences concerning degrees of relationship, where sexual intercourse is forbidden. Here a verb with a negative stands at the end. 'The nakedness of . . . you shall not uncover.'[2] Such

---

[1] On the casuistic element found here cf. E. GERSTENBERGER, *Wesen und Herkunft des sogenannten apodiktischen Rechts im Alten Testament*, Diss., Bonn, 1961.

[2] Cf. K. ELLIGER, 'Das Gesetz Leviticus 18', *ZAW* 67 (1955), pp. 1–25.

negative prohibitions are also found in a list naming persons who are to be reverenced or abhorred: 'You shall not permit a sorceress to live' (Exod. xxii. 18, Heb. 17). 'You shall not revile God. You shall not curse a ruler of your people' (Exod. xxii. 28, Heb. 27). The small handbook for behaviour in lawsuits of Exodus xxiii. 1–3, 6–9 must also be compared with this. Above all, the classical Decalogue must be considered here, although two of its prohibitions have been replaced by positive commandments (those concerning the sabbath and respect for parents). The formal similarity of the clauses has been largely lost in the Decalogue. The content of the Decalogue, in contrast to the laws detailed above which deal with special situations, shows an intention to encompass as wide an area of life as possible. Furthermore all stipulations of punishment are lacking. From the standpoint of form criticism the classical Decalogue does not represent a starting point. The desire to maintain a pure form has given way here in favour of the desire to obtain a greater coverage in content. For this purpose, therefore, evidently ten laws were selected from a number of particular commandments, which were already in existence, and which bore different forms.

When we ask what the *Sitz im Leben* is of such apodictic laws, we certainly cannot refer to the secular lay justice administered at the gate. The whole nature of such laws expresses a note of authority. They intrude into life from outside, and lay down commandments for it. Where then, do they belong? Deuteronomy xxvii shows that such series of curses belonged in a sacral act of the people of Israel. They were proclaimed by a priestly spokesman in the name of Yahweh, and the congregation answered with their 'Amen'. The use of the second person singular form of address, which occurs in the Decalogue, also expresses a note of authority. It is probable that Deuteronomy xxvii describes a rite which was celebrated regularly. Deuteronomy xxxi. 10–13 informs us that the law of God had to be read every seven years, in a great assembly of the people, at the Feast of Tabernacles in the sanctuary of Yahweh. According to the present text this law was that of Deuteronomy. Here a recurring celebration of the renewal of the covenant is recognizable, in which the proclamation of the law had its place. From this it immediately becomes understandable that the first great proclamation of the law of God by the mouth of Moses, or, as in the case of the Decalogue, from God's own mouth, originated in the context of the conclusion of the covenant of Israel on Mount Sinai. In our present Old Testament it is there that we find the Book of the

Covenant, and also the Decalogue, with its emphatic, 'I am Yahweh your God'.[1] In Psalm lxxxi we may well have a psalm belonging to the context of the Autumn Festival. Here Alt follows up a suggestion from Mowinckel's work on the law. The hymnic introduction in verses 1–5a (Heb. 2–6a) extends an invitation to the celebration of the feast, with the sound of musical instruments and songs. After a transition in verses 5b–8 (Heb. 6b–9), praising God's beneficent acts and declaring a summons to hear his word, there follows in verses 9–10 (Heb. 10–11) a fairly free quotation from the beginning of the Decalogue.

All of these facts make it very probable that in the apodictic law we have a form of law that was indigenous to Israel. The two great streams of law, however, the casuistic and the apodictic, soon became united. The Book of the Covenant, in which both streams can still be seen in a relatively pure form, is at the same time the document where both streams meet. Casuistic laws are here subordinate to the will of the great lawgiver, who created in the apodictic form his own distinctive form of expression. Scholarship still has here a large field of work before it, if it is to understand fully this process of amalgamation of the various laws. Alt's examination was intended to be a strictly legal-historical study, which would illuminate the origins of Israelite law. If we look back for a moment to Wellhausen's view of the development of law, we can see how much things have changed as a result of this new approach. Whilst Wellhausen is still correct in removing the cultic legislation of the Priestly Document from the time of Moses, it has nevertheless become evident that early Israel did not lack a formulated law. On the contrary, after Israel settled in the land, there began a lively process of interchange between different traditions of law, which was full of tension. Admittedly the law in the form given to it by the Priestly Document is later than the prophets, but the prophets themselves belonged to a people who traced their origin to the proclamation of the law. Not only were they familiar with it in the form of oral instruction of *torah*, as Wellhausen accepted, but as a divine law, formulated in awesome statutes and recited at regular intervals in the name of Yahweh.

At the same time, however, the problem of the Decalogue has been unexpectedly put in a wider perspective. The Decalogue no longer can be regarded as the unique achievement of the genius Moses, but as a series of commandments which stand beside other possible series, which

[1] W. Zimmerli, 'Ich bin Jahwe', *Festschrift A. Alt*, Tübingen, 1953, pp. 179–209; reprinted in *Gottes Offenbarung*, München, 1963, pp. 11–40.

are still in part recognizable. Admittedly this series is especially prominent because of its preamble expressing the divine self-disclosure, yet in its individual statutes it belongs together with other collections of laws. It must be examined form-critically, as a structure which may well have had purer and more ancient formulations lying behind it. At the same time it is certainly not a structure requiring for its development a previous prophetic phase of higher spirituality and elevated morality. The individual statutes reach back to an early phase of Israelite proclamation of law, although their combination in the present form as a series of ten may well have occurred after Moses.

Alt's work, however, was not only important for its historical results. Through its persistent search for the *Sitz im Leben* of Old Testament law, and through its more exact study of the origin of specifically Israelite law, it opened the way for a fresh examination of the significance of law as a whole. Monographs by G. von Rad[1] and M. Noth[2] have shown this more clearly. In his *Theologie des Alten Testaments* von Rad has further taken up the whole question of the theological understanding of law in the Old Testament.

Before moving on to the question of the meaning of the law, as it is raised in von Rad's theology, we may look briefly at the two works of von Rad and Noth referred to above.

As the title indicates, von Rad's *Das formgeschichtliche Problem des Hexateuch* examines the formation of the great narrative work from Genesis to Joshua which is now divided into six books. How did this huge narrative complex come into being, encompassing the primeval history, the patriarchal narratives, the story of the exodus with the extensive account of the events on Sinai, and then the history of the conquest under Joshua? Why precisely has the whole been given this structure? Von Rad discovered that the real kernel around which this lengthy narrative has crystallized is a short credo-like summary, telling briefly of the exodus of Israel from Egypt, and its entrance into the land of Canaan. It is found in a number of places, in psalms, narrative accounts, and most attractively in the liturgical prayer for a peasant bringing his first-fruits in thanksgiving for the harvest to the sanctuary (Deut. xxvi. 5–10). It is also evident in the preamble to the Decalogue, declaring the fundamental act of God towards Israel in the

[1] G. VON RAD, *Das formgeschichtliche Problem des Hexateuch*, Stuttgart, 1938; reprinted in *Gesammelte Studien zum A.T.*, München, 1958, pp. 9–86.

[2] M. NOTH, *Die Gesetze im Pentateuch*, Halle, 1940; reprinted in *Gesammelte Studien zum A.T.*, München, 1957, pp. 9–141.

manner of a credal statement. This is the centre around which other narratives have accumulated, and upon which they have crystallized. These covered the history of the age of the promise of God to the patriarchs, which prepared for the history of Israel, and the primeval history, which is prefaced to the whole. The seams which hold the complex together can still be clearly recognized.

It is quite striking that these brief credo-like summaries did not as a rule even mention the important events of the sojourn at Sinai. Thus we may conjecture that the formation of the account of the Sinai events has its own earlier tradition-history. This, however, says nothing about its historicity or its historical correlation with the event of the exodus, although it does necessitiate a separate consideration of the Sinai tradition as having its own character and centre of gravity. In the exodus tradition everything points towards the goal of the possession of the land, in which the narrative comes to rest, whilst in the Sinai account this migratory movement has completely disappeared. Exodus xix f. is concerned with preparing the people for their encounter with God, with the tremendous event of the theophany, which is bound up with the giving of the law, and then in chapter xxiv with the making of the covenant. Here von Rad accepts Mowinckel's conclusions, with slight modifications, and finds behind this great series of events the evidence of a festival, in which the major phases of its liturgical outline may still be seen in Exodus xix. 20 and 24. He sees this same outline reflected in Deuteronomy, with its sequence of parenesis, proclamation of law, covenant obligations and blessings and curses.

For our purpose it is sufficient to emphasize two things. Following somewhat different paths of study, von Rad also comes to the conclusion that the law in Israel did not simply exist as general religious knowledge, but had a very definite liturgical setting. From Joshua xxiv we can conjecture that the proclamation of the law took place at the sanctuary in Shechem. The curse dodecalogue of Deuteronomy xxvii also points there. The communication of the law was therefore connected with the celebration of the covenant which bound Israel to its God.

Secondly this report of the communication of the law has been built into the great account of the saving history of Yahweh with Israel. Thus the larger context which it now has declares that the making of the covenant and the giving of the law were set within the story of God's guidance of history, of which even the preamble of the Decalogue reminds us. This conclusion has considerable importance for the theological understanding of law.

Noth's study, *Die Gesetze im Pentateuch,* leads to a fairly similar position, First of all the study shows that the Old Testament laws were in no way related to the political organization of the state. Rather they were concerned with a community of men in which the common allegiance to Yahweh was constitutive. By recalling the exodus from Egypt and the conquest of Canaan, this community acknowledged its relationship to Yahweh. At the same time it was conscious also through this recollection of being different from the Canaanites, with whom Israel then lived together in one state. In pre-monarchic times Israel existed as a sacral tribal federation, which may be compared with the amphictyonies of Greece. This community regarded itself as founded on a covenant, and the Sinai narrative tells how this covenant was established. It was celebrated in regular feasts, which served to maintain its vitality, and the entire law of Israel had its basis here.

According to Noth a crisis occurred in the exile. At this time the prophets preached the ending of the covenant, and after the exile, the old covenant institution was not re-established. As a consequence the law came to stand in a very different position. It was no longer the ordinance which rested on the covenant established by God, but instead it became an absolute entity, divorced from history, and was itself the way of salvation. It was against this understanding of the law that Paul fought.

The question arises whether Noth has correctly assessed the post-exilic period. For our purpose, however, the positive conclusion is important, that initially the law was wholly related to the covenant, which was fundamental to it. This leads once again to the central question of the theological significance of the phenomenon of the law. It is this question that we must now examine.

IV. The Theological Relevance of the Law

IN the work of Martin Noth mentioned previously there arise two possible ways of understanding the Old Testament law, which appear side by side, or perhaps we should say, facing one another. Noth sees the law in the pre-exilic period as related to the sacral tribal covenant, which actualized Israel's election by Yahweh in regular celebrations of covenant renewal. In the post-exilic period, however, this covenant background was dropped. According to Noth the law now became an absolute entity, divorced from history, and expressing solely a demand upon Israel. Joachim Begrich, the Leipzig Old Testament scholar, who was killed in Italy during the last days of the Second World War, undertook a study of the notion 'covenant' in his last essay[1] From a quite different direction he arrived at an analogous antithesis for the understanding of the covenant. According to Begrich the actual ancient Israelite interpretation saw in the covenant a pure gift of grace which Yahweh, as the senior partner, granted to his people. Beside this there was the form inspired by the Canaanite notion of treaty, which must be regarded as a perversion of the original idea of covenant. Here the covenant becomes a contract between two partners who both undertake certain rights and obligations in a reckoning of mutual interest. The contributions of both Noth and Begrich lead directly to the theological question of how the covenant, and the law which is anchored to it, are to be dealt with in the framework of an Old Testament theology.

G. von Rad has taken up this question in his *Old Testament Theology*,[2] so that our consideration of this question, which is so important for a theological understanding of the Old Testament, can best be undertaken in examining this work.

In his first volume, which in its outline closely follows the major themes of the Hexateuch, von Rad deals with the divine revelation on Sinai. A special section considers the significance of the commandments. He stresses emphatically that the question how the will of God en-

---

[1] JOACHIM BEGRICH, 'Berit. Ein Beitrag zur Erfassung einer alttestamentlichen Denkform', *ZAW* 60, 1944, pp. 1–11.

[2] G. VON RAD, *Theologie des Alten Testaments*, I, München, 1957, II, München, 1960; Eng. trans. of Vol. I as *Old Testament Theology*, I, Edinburgh, 1962.

countered by Israel in the Decalogue is to be understood cannot be answered by making the Decalogue a completely independent entity. It must rather be seen, 'that it is the proclamation of the Decalogue to Israel which brings Israel's election into full realization'.[1] God took Israel to himself by the proclamation of his name, and the simultaneous announcement of his commandments. 'The proclamation of the law, as an embodiment of the divine will, is like a net cast over Israel. In it Israel's identification with Yahweh is made complete.'[2] The evaluation of the commandments must begin with their anchoring in the cult of the covenant renewal feast. From this it may be understood that Israel regarded the communication of the commandments as a saving event. It is precisely in the commandment that the covenant becomes actual. The commandment is not therefore a conditional presupposition of the covenant. The covenant does not first come into effect through the keeping of the commandments, but rather, because the covenant exists, the commandments are proclaimed as Yahweh's ordinances. Thus the commandments are not 'law' in the strict theological sense. This can be seen also in the predominantly negative formulation of the commandments. 'The Decalogue lacks the most important element: a positive completeness, without which the law is hardly thinkable.'[3] The series of commandments do not have the intention of outlining a complete ethical system. They do not comprise Yahweh's maximum requirements. Only on the negative side, as an absolute minimum, do they give the mark of who belongs to Yahweh. He must not commit adultery, he must not steal, nor commit murder. In certain borderline situations the commandments demand a confession of allegiance to Yahweh, which is their purpose. Thus the law was thought of as something which could be easily fulfilled. Its observance was unconditionally demanded, as the threat of a curse for the disobedient makes clear. The motivation, which is occasionally added to the commandments, shows further that Yahweh's demand was regarded as completely reasonable.

It is even more important to realize that Israel did not regard God's demand as something rigidly frozen, but as requiring further interpretation. In the Holiness Code we see repeatedly how the commandments, which were originally formulated negatively, were expanded through positive summaries. Thus we find in Leviticus xix. 17 f.: 'You shall not hate your brother in your heart, but you shall reason with your neighbour, lest you bear sin because of him. You shall not take vengeance or bear any grudge against the sons of your own people, but

[1] Ibid., p. 192.   [2] Ibid.   [3] Ibid., p. 194.

you shall love your neighbour as yourself.' The commandment is flexible, and keeps pace with history precisely because it is a part of Yahweh's historical concern, which is constantly celebrated anew.

This tendency towards a summarizing interpretation is found most impressively in Deuteronomy. The demand for love to Yahweh with the whole heart and soul is prefaced to the detailed statement of the individual commandments (Deut. vi. 4 ff.). Deuteronomy is, in general, the book where the attempt is made most strongly to reflect upon God's demands in their wider setting. Von Rad refers to this in connection with his examination of Deuteronomy. In Deuteronomy the whole revelation of the divine will can be comprehensively designated as *torah*. As we have already seen this expression had its original home in connection with the priestly-cultic instruction. The introductory parenesis in Deuteronomy i–xi, which precedes the description of the law, elucidates the place of *torah* in a special way. If Israel keeps the *torah* she remains within the covenant. The covenant is thereby understood as almost synonymous with the love of Yahweh. Thus Israel must respond to Yahweh with its love above all else. Von Rad certainly establishes that there are in Deuteronomy occasional formulations which make the blessings of salvation conditional upon the obedience of Israel. 'Do this that you may live, that it may go well with you, that you may enter into the land.'[1] Yet even here, however, the background presupposition is that salvation and the covenant are real and actual.

In the post-exilic period, however, the law was made into something absolute, and was separated from history. In this von Rad follows the view of Noth. Israel now entered into the realm of 'law', against which the New Testament had to proclaim its new message.

At this point, however, von Rad has a further series of observations, standing rather unevenly with the foregoing, according to which the law emerged in a particularly legalistic understanding still some considerable time before the exile. We must mention here the second volume of von Rad's *Old Testament Theology*, which first deals with the prophets, and then deals in a later chapter, under the heading 'The Law', with the understanding of law in the Old Testament. Here once again, with considerable emphasis, von Rad stresses that Ancient Israel, which heard the law recited in the covenant festival, was in no way set in a situation of legalism. With regard to the Deuteronomic parenesis von Rad establishes, 'Israel's state of salvation was not threatened by the

[1] Ibid., p. 230.

law. The concern of this parenesis is not that Israel may not be able to fulfil the law, but rather that it may not be willing to do so.'[1]

There was, however, the fact of prophecy. The prophets recognized a new period of God's dealings with Israel. Judgments fell upon Israel in which an appeal to the old bases of salvation was no longer effective, because, in this new divine event, the question of the very existence or non-existence of Israel was at stake. Thus it is the first task of the prophets, 'that they employ every means of rhetoric and argumentation to shake their contemporaries out of their fixed and illusory possession of salvation. This they accomplish by proclaiming God's wrath to them, and by placing them under God's law. This independence of the preaching of the law, as also the great intensification of the proclamation of God's demand which threatens the very life of man, is something quite new.'[2]

In details von Rad makes a certain distinction between the prophets of the eighth century and those of the seventh and sixth centuries. The earlier group charges the people with the transgression of certain concrete commandments, but even more important is the charge that Israel has rebelled against the very saving action of God. The prophets of the eighth century certainly preached 'law'. They revealed sin, 'but this sin became apparent only in relation to God's acts of salvation, and not in relation to a juristic law which stood over against this saving activity'.[3] Not until the prophets of the seventh and sixth centuries do we find explicit consideration of the law. Jeremiah and Ezekiel occasionally hint at the idea that Israel is by nature incapable of obeying Yahweh. With them concrete individual commandments are mentioned which Israel has disobeyed. 'Here an actual law is mentioned, and the question of the fulfilment of this law is raised. The result of this inquiry is the terse statement that Israel has not fulfilled these requirements.'[4] Thus right at the point where the vision of a new God-given future emerges, the question of the possibility of fulfilling the law becomes apparent. Jeremiah xxxi. 31 ff. proclaims the new covenant in which the law will be written in the hearts of Israel. Similarly Ezekiel xxxvi. 26 ff. speaks of the new heart which enables the people to fulfil the commandments.

When we examine the deeper motives for this obviously new understanding of the law, we may consider what von Rad says of Amos, who confronted his people directly with the ancient demand of God: 'The

[1] Ibid., p. 407.   [2] Ibid., p. 409.
[3] Ibid., p. 411.   [4] Ibid., p. 413.

surprising feature is that Amos took these ordinances with such uncompromising seriousness at a time which had long since cast off any
relationship to them.'[1] At this point we may go further and ask
whether, by taking the ancient law so seriously, the prophet does not
simply fulfil its intention. If this is the case, does his preaching of judgment then not reveal a real threat, which already lay hidden in the old
commandment? For von Rad, however, another factor is of greater
importance. He believes that he is able to find in the prophets more
frequent examples of a 'bold reinterpretation of the old ordinance,'
which can only be understood charismatically'.[2] Thus he sees in the
use made of the first and second commandments (the prohibition of
images) against the syncretism of the period of the monarchy, such a
bold extension of their original meaning. 'In view of the eschatological
situation, the prophets face the task of interpreting anew from the old
ordinances what Yahweh requires of Israel here and now.' The distinctive feature of the prophetic preaching of the law consisted in their
application of the law of Israel to the peoples surrounding it, and con-
sequently to the whole world. Even more than this, however, the
prophets were distinctive because of 'the radical nature of this preaching of the law, and the vehemence with which they uncovered even the
most secret areas of life, and set them in the light of the divine demand'.[3]
They no longer simply condemn isolated transgressions, and announce
God's punishment to individual transgressors, but they speak of the
failure of the entire nation. Von Rad sees in this the 'bold interpretation' of the prophets, in that they fought so inexorably to establish the
failure of the entire nation on the grounds of the ancient norms of the
sacral law of Yahweh. The theological justification for this interpretation, in which, in von Rad's opinion, the content of the old law was
transcended, is solely to be found in the charismatic authority of these
men. We may also ask here whether by this interpretation they remain
within the reality of the covenant which the commandments sought
to maintain, or whether they broke away from this by their radical
interpretation, and took up a new position.

I have given considerable space to the view of von Rad, because it
is of great importance as an attempt to undertake once again, as pene-
tratingly as possible, a full theological examination of what the New
Testament understands by the key-word 'law'. This was a fundamental issue both for the New Testament and for the Reformation.

A further reason for giving space to the presentation of von Rad's

[1] Ibid., p. 414.   [2] Ibid.   [3] Ibid., p. 415.

work is because it leads, from a slightly different direction, to the heart of our problem, namely the question of the law and the prophets. Von Rad's presentation makes possible a quite new view of their relationship, which may surprise us. Briefly formulated it may be stated that von Rad endeavours to make clear how the oldest law, which the work of Alt has shown to be a constituent part of Ancient Israel, is not 'law' in the theological sense. On the contrary it is the prophets who preached 'law'. Roughly stated we can say that 'Moses', i.e. the preacher of the old law, became the 'Moses' of the evangelists, whilst it is the prophets who became the 'Moses' of Paul.

The theological discussion of the law in the Old Testament is thus raised once again. How shall we consider the view proposed by von Rad? First we must note that von Rad's discussion of the law is not free from a certain obscurity. Besides what is said of the prophets as preachers of the law we have a reference, taken over by von Rad from Noth, to the law of the later period, as something that was understood quite independently of any history. The question arises as to how these two concepts of the law are related to each other. We might go further and ask whether there is at all in the Old Testament such a concept of law separated from the covenant on the one hand, and from history on the other. We may suppose that on this point a strong objection could be raised by Jewish Old Testament scholars, and perhaps rightly so. For the present I shall leave out this question completely. It would especially lead us into the third part of the canon, the Writings, to the Psalms, the work of the Chronicler and the book of Daniel. We may limit ourselves here to the phenomenon of the law, which is found in the older Old Testament literature, the Law and the Prophets. Here in the ancient laws of Israel von Rad does not find 'law' in the theological sense of the word, whilst on his view the prophets were preachers of such a 'law'. This prescribes for us the course of our further examination. We must first examine carefully once again the older laws to see whether they are 'law', and afterwards do the same with the message of the prophets.

Before we do so, however, there is another preliminary question. What is meant by 'law' in the deepest theological sense? Our discussion up to now should have made it clear that 'law' is a commandment which has the power to expel men, or even the whole nation of Israel, from the covenant. We may state it in accordance with the New Testament by saying that 'law' is related to the curse (Gr. *katara*).[1]

---

[1] Gal. iii. 13.

Another New Testament definition says that the law can lead to boasting (Gr. *kauchesis*). We shall keep to the first definition in what follows, and consider the question of the relationship between law and curse.

For this purpose we must once again refer to the covenant, in which the Old Testament commandment is embedded. The essay of Begrich, which we mentioned previously, outlined very clearly two different ways of understanding the covenant. There was the idea of the covenant as a pure gift of grace in which a senior partner unconditionally conferred upon a junior partner the saving relationship of a covenant out of his own free grace (cf. 1 Sam. xviii. 3 f., the covenant of Jonathan with David). Secondly there was the covenant of contract which was made between two parties on specific conditions. Begrich's examination proceeded entirely from the Hebrew terminology of covenant making. Both Noth and von Rad show undeniably an understanding of the covenant in the first sense of Begrich's covenant of grace.

In recent years the phenomenon of the covenant has been illuminated by all kinds of newly discovered materials from the environment of Israel. Thus Noth has demonstrated from the Mari texts[1] a form of covenant in which a third person negotiated a covenant between two contending parties with a special ritual of the slaughtering of an ass. He has raised the question whether the Hebrew *berith* (= covenant) may not be explained from the Accadian *biritu* (= between), which occurs in the description of the covenant.

In this connection we must note another analogy, which shows in its individual elements a remarkable similarity to the Old Testament covenant, even though the historical ways by which the connection could have come about are still completely obscure. This is to be found in a group of state treaties, the so-called suzerainty treaties, which the Hittite kings concluded with dependent princes. The texts have been published in various places. In 1931 a lawyer, V. Korošec, edited them,[2] and, after Hempel referred to them in the second edition of *Die Religion in Geschichte und Gegenwart* in the article on 'covenant', they have more recently been given a very full attention.[3]

---

[1] M. NOTH, 'Das alttestamentliche Bundschliessen im Lichte eines Mari-Textes', *Annuaire de l'institut de philologie et d'histoire orientales et slaves*, XIII, 1955, pp. 433–44; reprinted in *Gesammelte Studien zum A.T.*, München, 1957, pp. 142–54.

[2] V. KOROŠEC, *Hethitische Staatsverträge. Ein Beitrag zu ihrer juristischen Wertung*, Leipziger rechtswissenschaftliche Studien 60, Leipzig, 1931.

[3] G. E. MENDENHALL, 'Covenant Forms in Israelite Tradition', *BA* 17, 1954, pp. 50–76; K. BALTZER, *Das Bundesformular*, Neukirchen, 1960; see also the unpublished dissertation by G. HEINEMANN *Untersuchung zum apodiktischen Recht*.

These texts are characteristically introduced by a historical prologue which narrates the history leading up to the conclusion of the covenant. Thus, for example, the Hittite emperor Muršiliš reminds vassal Kapanta-KAL, in a treaty, that he, the emperor, graciously confirmed and defended Kapanta-KAL as king, although the latter's uncle, who had adopted him as successor, had been disloyal to the emperor. Therefore it was an act of pure grace which the Hittite emperor had shown to his vassal in making him king. This history is preceded by a preamble which gives the names and title of the ruler conferring the covenant. After these two introductory elements there follow the particular stipulations of the covenant. Baltzer believes that there is at the centre first of all a basic description of the future relationship of the two partners. Thus it says in another treaty, 'Now guard the king's oath and authority; I, the sun, will protect you, Duppi-Teshub ... and do not look to another'.[1] Then follow the concrete stipulations to the vassals. This section of commandments constitutes the major portion of the treaty. In it we read regulations concerning the relationship to other powers, trade questions, military problems, the extradition of refugees, prisoners of war, payments of tribute, 'arrogance', etc. Then follows on the part of the overlord the promise of protection and an assurance of the right of succession to the throne. In a suzerainty treaty of the Assyrian sovereign Esarhaddon, the structure of which differs from the others at many points, we find in this section, 'Observe this treaty and do not break your covenant lest you forfeit your life.'[2] In connection with the Old Testament the condition that follows in yet another Hittite treaty is surprising, 'The tablet that I have written out for you, Alakshandush, which should be read to you three times every year, and you, Alakshandush, should know it'.[3] Then follow the concluding elements: the appeal to the gods as witnesses to the treaty, which may be followed by detailed lists of gods. Finally we have the threat of the curse in the case of non-observance, and the promise of blessing when the ordinances are kept. 'If you, Alakshandush, break these words of the document ... then these oaths will destroy you yourself, your wife, your sons, and they will destroy your seed from off the black earth. If, however, you keep these words, then these

[1] K. BALTZER, op. cit., p. 223.

[2] D. J. WISEMAN, *The Vassal-Treaties of Esarhaddon*, London, 1958, pp. 52, 291-3.

[3] J. FRIEDRICH, 'Staatsverträge des Hatti-Reiches in Hethitischer Sprache', *MVAG* 34, Leipzig, 1930, pp. 50 ff. (sections 19, 73-75); K. BALTZER, op. cit., p. 28.

thousand gods, the gods of Hatti, will graciously protect you, your wife, your sons, and your grandchildren. In the hand of the sun (the emperor) may you see good fortune, and in the hand of the sun become old.'[1]

We see in these vassal-treaties a specific type of covenant which is connected with the proclamation of a covenant law. Its distinctiveness is that the covenant is described in a historical preamble as the result of the gracious attitude of the sovereign. This is reminiscent of the preamble of the Decalogue, and of the introductory speeches of Deuteronomy. The statutes of the treaty are then authoritatively asserted. It is clear that their observance is decisive for the continuing validity of the covenant, and at the conclusion they are guaranteed by words of blessing and curse. This is strongly reminiscent of the closing chapters of Deuteronomy (Deut. xxviii ff.), and of the Holiness Code (Lev. xxvi) with their assertion of blessings and curses. This injunction that the document is to be read regularly is also a striking parallel to Deuteronomy xxxi. 10 ff.

Is this type of covenant one of grace or one of contract? Obviously the question cannot be put as a clear-cut choice between two such sharply defined alternatives, since elements of both are combined here. There is a reference to the beneficent giving of the sovereign, and an account of his favourable actions. At the same time, however, whilst these treaties are clearly presented as the fruits of a genuine beneficence towards the vassals, there can be no doubt that their validity is dependent on the obedience of the latter. 'If Duppi-Teshub does not keep these words of the treaty and oath, then may these oaths destroy Duppi-Teshub himself, his wife . . . his city, his land.'[2] The oaths sworn over the covenant seem here like independent powers, which execute judgment on the covenant-breaker if necessary.

Even if all historical questions are left open, the consideration of these parallels at least raises the question whether the covenant of which Israel spoke, and in which Yahweh's commands were embedded, might not be similar to these treaties. Could it not be the case with Israel's covenant that the threat to the partner who had not kept the covenant ordinance might arise directly from the nature of the covenant itself? Thus the commandment preached to Israel was not only a net in which the people were unexpectedly snared by Yahweh,[3] but was the accuser, the source of the curse which fell upon the people. From the divine standpoint are we to say that Yahweh's word, given to Israel

[1] J. FRIEDRICH, op. cit., section 21, 31–46.
[2] K. BALTZER, op. cit., p. 191.   [3] See above page 47.

in his commandments, is only a word of grace which upholds the people at any price, or is it not rather a holy fire, by which the unholy could be consumed, and Israel rejected?

The literature on the law must be examined again with this question in mind. We have the Book of the Covenant, which, as the present text of Exodus xxiv shows, is clearly related to the covenant. Unfortunately this chapter gives no further information as to how the commandments were related to the purpose of the covenant. Even the content of this legal code is remarkably reserved on this point. The book lacks any preamble which might shed light on its theological significance. As we have already mentioned, in the laws themselves different types of divine commands stand side by side with little attempt to weld them together. In the apodictic laws we cannot mistake the authoritative will of a master. In the series dealing with capital crimes the phrase, 'He shall be put to death' occurs with almost monotonous regularity, showing that this authoritative will has complete power over life and death. It is possible therefore for a man to fall by it. Thus when, in particular, God demands a respect for the weak, the law adds, 'My wrath will burn, and I will kill you with the sword, and your wives shall become widows and your children fatherless' (Exod. xxii. 24, Heb. 23). Here it is clearly stated that disobedience towards Yahweh's commandment will bring death. These, however, are only incidental references. In the epilogue Exodus xxiii. 20–33 we have a description of the future blessings which God intends for his people. It is also said regarding the angel through whom God will lead the people on their journey, 'Give heed to him and hearken to his voice, do not rebel against him, for he will not pardon your transgression; for my name is in him' (Exod. xxiii. 21). The concern here is no longer for particular commandments; nevertheless it is clear that rebellion against God's messenger could mean the death of the people. It is precisely this nearness of God to his people, here mediated by his angel, which takes on a threatening aspect for those who are blessed by it.

In the curse dodecalogue of Deuteronomy xxvii. 15–26 we found a complete series of apodictic commands. Dressed in a Deuteronomic garment, there can be seen old legal formulations which may once have been connected with Shechem, as its introduction (vv. 1–8) states. The situation of the making of the covenant and the giving of the law can be clearly seen in the remarkably brief statement of verses 9–10, 'Keep silence and hear, O Israel; this day you have become the people of Yahweh your God. You shall therefore obey the voice of

Yahweh your God, keeping his commandments and his statutes, which I command this day.' When the tribes are subsequently divided into two groups of six, the one group to pronounce blessing from Mount Gerizim, and the other to pronounce a curse from Mount Ebal, we must also connect this scene with the giving of the law, and recall that already in the Hittite treaties the hypothetical proclamation of curse and blessing followed the covenant law. The sequence is here reversed, but the Hittite treaties clearly give the key to this dodecalogue of curses, which the Levites pronounce, and to which the people answer 'Amen'. Acts done secretly, which represent crimes beyond the scope of public justice, are here set under the curse of Yahweh. A series of particular commandments shows concretely how inseparably the law is connected, not only with blessing, but also with a possible curse. This curse is certainly not directed only against those who stand outside the covenant. The very people who stand within the covenant are those addressed here. Law is therefore not simply an occasion to confess Yahweh in marginal situations.[1] It can also become unexpectedly the place where the curse takes effect within the covenant community. Whether or not this curse could one day directly threaten the covenant itself is undoubtedly not contemplated here. However a deeper reflection must consider this question. One of the curses states, 'Cursed be he who removes his neighbour's landmark'. What happens then if the rulers of the whole nation remove boundary marks, as Hosea v. 10 asserts, 'The princes of Judah have become like those who remove the landmark'? Is the threat which Hosea then formulates: 'Upon them I will pour out my wrath like water', not a curse pronounced against the whole people? If so is this not already included in the curse of Deuteronomy xxvii. 17?

We must now consider the classic series of ten commandments contained in Exodus xx, which are probably an ancient legal formulation of purely Israelite origin. The series has an explicit preamble which mentions the lawgiver, showing from whom it derives. The basic element of the preamble is a sentence of God's self-disclosure, 'I am Yahweh'. This is the speech of someone stepping out of the mystery of obscurity, who is prepared to make himself known to another person. It is characteristic of God's speeches, which are frequently to be found in the theophanies described in Genesis. In the Decalogue this self-disclosure is related to the celebration of the covenant festival, in which an authorized spokesman confronted the people in the name of

[1] See above page 47.

Yahweh, and in that name announced to them the divine law. We should like to know more about this process. We have already mentioned that Psalms l and lxxxi show this event taking place in one of the festivals of the community.[1]

The self-disclosure does not stop, however, with the simple announcement of Yahweh's name, but makes an addition which defines who Yahweh is more exactly, 'I am Yahweh your God, who brought you out of the land of Egypt, out of the house of bondage'. The proclamation of the law comes from the mouth of God who introduces himself to Israel as 'your God', that is as the God of the covenant. The covenant is not a mythical primordial datum for Israel, but rests on a historical act of liberation, which the credo outlines, as we have already discovered. Just as the preamble of the Hittite treaties described the history of the appointment of the vassals to their ruling position as an act of grace, so we have here the description of Israel's deliverance and elevation to her present position as an act of Yahweh's grace. The god who has dealt so graciously with Israel, now announces to Israel his law and commandment.

After this straightforward beginning, however, a complication occurs. After the first two commandments of the Decalogue there follows a second identification of Yahweh as the motivation for a law, 'For I Yahweh your God am a jealous God, visiting the iniquity of the fathers upon the children to the third and fourth generation of those who hate me, but showing steadfast love to thousands of those who love me and keep my commandments'.[2] The beginning could also be translated, 'For I am Yahweh your God, a jealous God'. In this motive clause God introduces himself once again, or perhaps we should say, his original introduction is expanded by a fuller description. Yahweh, who has liberated his people, is also the jealous God who does not tolerate that other gods should receive the love and adoration of his people.

The second self-disclosure does not take place simply with words adopted on the spur of the moment, but rather we can see here an important formulation, probably used repeatedly as an ascription of God in cultic ceremonies. Possibly we have in the Yahwist's description of Yahweh's revelation to Moses on Mount Sinai, contained in Exodus

[1] See above page 35.
[2] The insertion of the second formula of introduction represents a later stage of development in the transmission of the text. However, in any case, it shows the pre-exilic interpretation of the law.

xxxiv. 6 f., an authentic echo of the name of Yahweh given to Moses:
'Yahweh Yahweh, a God merciful and gracious, slow to anger, and
abounding in steadfast love and faithfulness, keeping steadfast love for
thousands, forgiving iniquity and transgression and sin, but who will
by no means clear the guilty, visiting the iniquity of the fathers upon
the children and the children's children, to the third and the fourth
generation'. The formula is repeated in the prayer of Moses in Numbers xiv. 18, and in the Deuteronomic parenesis of Deuteronomy vii. 9 f.

The reference to the punishing of guilt to the third and fourth
generation presumably stems from the law commanding the destruction of certain persons and property which are placed under Yahweh's
ban (Heb. *ḥerem*). Four generations, to which the formula probably
originally referred, is the maximum number of generations that can
be found together in one family (great grandmother, grandmother,
mother and child). Thus we hear in the account of the blessing of
Joseph that he even saw his great grandchildren (Gen. l. 23, corrected
text). With the execution of Achan (Joshua vii. 24 ff.) the family is
executed with him. In such a context the formula of inflicting a punishment to the third and fourth generations means the total destruction of
an entire family. With this severity the wrath of God burns against
those who transgress the commandments. Thus we hear in Deuteronomy vi. 15, immediately after the admonition that Israel is to
have no other gods, 'For Yahweh your God in the midst of you is a
jealous God; lest the anger of Yahweh your God be kindled against
you, and he destroy you from off the face of the earth'. (Cf. also
Deut. iv. 24.)

We now see how this formula is connected with the other statement
that Yahweh is merciful, gracious and forgiving; and indeed that he
honours his covenant to the thousandth generation. In this statement
the original significance of the four-generation formula is broken, since
a household which encompasses a thousand generations is unthinkable.
The intention is to show that God's grace is even stronger than his
wrath, and that Yahweh desires the life and not the death of his people.
Nevertheless it is certainly not that the one is swallowed up in the
other. Both stand side by side; the formula of punishment, for which
perhaps the word 'curse' would be better, and the formula of grace.
The God who seeks the welfare of his people is at the same time their
judge.

Thus by the preaching of the law Israel comes to stand in a unique
position. The declaration of God's law recalls his great act of grace

towards them. They are the property of a God who is patient and gracious, and who seeks to bless them. At the same time they are the property of a God who is zealous for his will, and who cannot tolerate that his people should disobey him.

This becomes still clearer from other references. Joshua xxiv describes a great assembly at Shechem, at the very place where the proclamation of the law of God to Israel was firmly established. According to the present text Joshua challenged the people to decide whether they would serve their God. A parenetic introduction recalls all the gracious acts which they had been shown by their God (vv. 2–15). The people then declare themselves ready to serve Yahweh (vv. 16–18). Joshua answers, 'You cannot serve Yahweh; for he is a holy God; he is a jealous God; he will not forgive your transgressions or your sins. If you forsake Yahweh and serve foreign gods, then he will turn and do you harm, and consume you, after having done you good' (Joshua xxiv. 19 f.). However, since the people insisted upon their decision, Joshua concluded a covenant on that day, declaring both statute and law to the people. He instructed them in the commandments of Yahweh, wrote them in a book (this is perhaps a later expansion), and erected a huge stone with the words, 'Behold, this stone shall be a witness against us; for it has heard all the words of Yahweh which he spoke to us; therefore it shall be a witness against you, lest you deal falsely with your God' (Joshua xxiv. 27). We are reminded of the Hittite treaties which, in their conclusion, summon witnesses (in their case a number of gods), so that they might guard the law of the covenant. Here too we see how Israel is brought into a great blessing, because it is bound to its God, who has dealt so graciously with it. At the same time, however, it becomes clear that it also stands under the possibility of wrath, which could befall it, if it abandons its God. The stone serves as a witness of this.

Also in the later law books of Deuteronomy and the Holiness Code (Lev. xvii–xxvi) we see that they conclude with blessings and curses, sharply outlined, and set side by side as two possibilities as in the Hittite treaties. In Leviticus xxvi. 25 we find in this connection a unique reference to 'a sword that shall execute vengeance for the covenant', which will be sent against the people if they are disobedient. Evil does not come from outside, but directly from the covenant itself, and befall a people who do not obey the law which the covenant contains.

It is quite impossible to unite systematically the two lines of expression which already appear together in the Decalogue, and which also

recur in the later law books. They must be plainly recognized side by
side in a state of tension. On the one hand we have the affirmation of
the covenant, concluded on the basis of Yahweh's free grace, in which
forgiveness has its place, and in which Yahweh upholds his people. In
this regard we may mention the promise which was made to the
patriarchs, and all the help which Israel had received from its God in its
history, including his intervention in the holy war. On the other hand
we have the affirmation of the law, and of the holy God who is jealous
for his commandments, and who threatens the people who do not
remain loyal to him. Already the ancient narratives of the wandering
in the wilderness show a knowledge of such a threat, which even at that
time brought Israel very close to destruction.

It is undoubtedly wrong to characterize the Israel of the Old Testament as a people who, in their faith, stood under a threatening law.[1] It
is, however, equally wrong to present the covenant people of the Old
Testament as a people whose faith led them to believe that they were
secure in the covenant from any radical threat to life, and who regarded
the law solely as a call to show allegiance to Yahweh. This appears in
the work of Noth, and more clearly still in that of von Rad. The law
stands rather as something, which hides a curse behind it, even though,
because of its connection with the covenant, it recalls God's great act
of salvation, and so is continually a reason for rejoicing. The God of
Israel, by whose gracious attitude the faith of the Old Testament lives,
always remains inexorable in his will. In the tension between these two
affirmations Ancient Israel lived.

It is in this setting that prophecy arose, and it is to this that we must
now turn.

---

[1] As, for example, E. HIRSCH, *Das Alte Testament und die Predigt des Evangeliums*,
Tübingen, 1936.

V. The Prophets down to the Eighth Century

WE have been considering the law, which in Israel cannot be separated from the covenant. As we continue we come once again to the prophets. Recent scholarship has shown clearly that it is wrong to regard the prophets as revolutionaries, who, as free creative personalities, ushered in a new age of moral understanding. Rather it has become clear that the prophets appeared in an Israel which had long been familiar with the preaching of its distinctive divine law. 'Such a thing is not done in Israel' (2 Sam. xiii. 12). By this ancient formula Israel confessed that it was aware of being different from its environment. What the law of God forbids is spoken of as 'folly in Israel' (Gen. xxxiv. 7; Deut. xxii. 21; Joshua vii. 15; Judges xx. 6; cf. 2 Sam. xiii. 13; Jer. xxix. 23).

We must, therefore, ask now whether the words of the prophets show that they stood in relation to the law and the covenant. Were the prophets concerned specifically with the divine law, which belonged to the covenant between Yahweh and Israel? If they were, did they say anything which is specially relevant to the theological significance of law?

The beginnings of Israelite prophecy remain obscure. It may be sufficient here to point out that in the period of the formation of the Israelite state we meet two phenomenologically different types of prophecy. On the one side there were the enthusiastic bands of charismatic prophets. In the Egyptian tale of Wen-Amon such a mantic prophet appears in Byblos,[1] which raises the question whether such prophecy might not have been introduced into Israel from Canaan. I Samuel x describes a band of such prophets, who came down from the high-place of Gibeah with music and instruments, and drew the young Saul into their ecstatic behaviour. They appear to have been closely connected with the cult. The groups of temple singers, Asaph, Heman, Jeduthun, whose playing is described in 1 Chronicles xxv. 1–3 as 'prophesying' (Heb. *hinnabe'*), could have been the later heirs of this type of cultic prophecy. On the other side the older historical narratives show that there were also individuals who were approached for advice on difficult matters, or who were able to give spontaneous

[1] *ANET*, pp. 25–29.

advice, because they received a superhuman knowledge from God. In the past these figures have been compared with the Arabian *kahin*.[1] More recently the Mari texts have shown the existence of persons who gave spontaneous advice under divine authorization, who may be seen as the forerunners of the Israelite prophets.[2] In the older period of Israel the individuals who gave spontaneous advice such as Samuel (1 Sam. ix f.) appear rather to have been termed 'seers' (so 1 Sam. ix. 9).

When the prophets of the later period are examined about the nature of their office, they do not point back to this earlier history. The form-critical study of the prophetic preaching shows that the prophet regarded himself as the messenger of Yahweh, who had to deliver the decision of his God and the announcement of a divine action. The preaching of the prophet is frequently introduced by the so-called message-formula, 'Thus says Yahweh',[3] or originally perhaps more exactly, 'Thus has Yahweh spoken'. Genesis xxxii. 4 f. demonstrates the way in which this introductory formula was originally used. Jacob here sends messengers to his brother Esau, with the instruction, 'Thus you shall say to my lord Esau: Thus says your servant Jacob, I have sojourned with Laban, and stayed until now; and I have oxen, asses, flocks, menservants and maidservants; and I have sent to tell my lord, in order that I may find favour in your sight.' The words, with which the messengers are to introduce their speech to those who hear it, point back to the moment when they themselves received it from the one who has sent them. They must repeat what was told to them at that time. Similarly the prophet knows that he has been sent from the moment when he received his message. Jeremiah xxiii. 21 ff. makes it clear that the prophet was allowed to stand in the divine council, and that he heard in it what God had resolved, and was being sent with this message.

We must ask now whether the prophet in Israel, who was commissioned by God with his message, shows that he regarded himself as a messenger of the covenant, which was characterized by the law of God

[1] Cf. G. Hölscher, *Die Profeten*, pp. 79 ff.

[2] A. Lods, 'Une tablette inédite de Mari, intéressante pour l'histoire ancienne du prophétisme sémitique', *Studies in Old Testament Prophecy*, ed. H. H. Rowley, Edinburgh, 1950, pp. 103 ff.; W. von Soden, 'Verkündigung des Gotteswillens durch prophetisches Wort in den altbabylonischen Briefen aus Mari', *WdO*, 1950, pp. 397 ff.; M. Noth, 'History and the Word of God in the Old Testament', *BJRL* 32, 1949/50, pp. 194 ff.

[3] L. Köhler, *Deuterojesaia (Jes. 40–55), stilkritisch untersucht (BZAW 37)*, Giessen, 1923, pp. 102–9.

proclaimed within it. In the Former Prophets (Joshua–2 Kings), there are a number of stories of the earlier prophets. They are, however, always narrated in the third person, sometimes after a great lapse of time. It is sufficient for our purpose to select from these narratives the accounts of two of the older prophets, Nathan and Elijah. We can then give fuller attention to the Latter Prophets, where we have the prophet's own words.

We have little information about Nathan, who lived at the court of King David, and we know neither his origin, nor his father's name. Twice, however, we see how he appeared with an important prophetic message. 2 Samuel vii reports that Nathan, on Yahweh's authority, opposed the plans of David to build a house for Yahweh. At the same time he promised David that Yahweh intended to build for him a house (i.e. dynasty). Unlike Saul's kingship, which disappeared with Saul's death, David was promised that God intended to give his house permanence, and would regard David's descendants as his sons. In this promise undoubtedly many elements of an older, pre-Israelite-Canaanite, royal tradition were taken up. When we set this promise in the wider context of the promise of God to Israel, we can see that it expresses a new, and hitherto unknown, demonstration of the gracious attitude of God to his people and their king. This history of Yahweh's saving action towards Israel was thereby continued. The prophetic promise subsequently came to take on a unique historical significance, and shaped the history of Judah in a particular way. It became the basis on which arose eventually the messianic expectation of the truly righteous descendant of David. In the prophecies of Isaiah of Jerusalem we can see the outworking of this new promise given through Nathan.

Soon afterwards there follows in 2 Samuel xii a second, and entirely different, meeting between David and Nathan. In order to conceal his adultery with the wife of his warrior Uriah, David arranged Uriah's death in battle. Later David took Bathsheba, the wife of Uriah as his wife. Then Nathan confronted David in the name of Yahweh, and narrated to him the story of a rich man, who had many sheep, but who stole the lamb of his poor neighbour. With this story he evoked David's impulsive judgment, 'The man who has done this deserves to die'. Nathan then replied, 'You are the man', and announced to David the death of the child, who was to be born from the marriage to Bathsheba.

'You shall not commit adultery . . . You shall not kill.' Thus commands the Decalogue in which God also stated that he is a zealous God. The curse which is theoretically connected with the law appears here openly in the word of the prophet which announces the death of the child. Even the king is a member of the covenant people. Thus the curse of the law turns against him.

In a later period we find the prophet Elijah contending against Ahab and Jezebel (1 Kings xvii ff.). The worship of foreign deities in the land, on the part of a foreign princess, seems to have been taken as a naturally accepted diplomatic courtesy in the days of Solomon. The prophet Elijah withstood this practice in the name of the first commandment. Once again in another incident he opposed the king (1 Kings xxi). Ahab wanted to buy the vineyard of Naboth, a Jezreelite, in order to round out the palace grounds. After Naboth had refused him, Jezebel, who, as a Tyrian princess had her own conception of a king's authority, proceeded to have Naboth killed on the grounds that he had blasphemed God and the king. Nathan's property fell to the crown, but once again the prophet came on the scene and met the king on Naboth's land. 'Have you killed and also taken possession?' The Decalogue proclaimed in Israel, 'You shall not kill. . . . You shall not covet your neighbour's house.' Again the prophet is the authorized messenger of God, who here announces a sentence of death on Ahab. When later Ahab's son Joram was killed by Jehu, and Ahab's house was destroyed, then Jehu recalled Elijah's word against Ahab (2 Kings ix. 26). Once again we find the prophet with his message as the guardian of the divine law. In his preaching we find a curse, bringing death, arising out of the commandment which has been trangressed. In this case the law is from the Decalogue, and the curse brings down an entire dynasty.

We must now turn to the so-called writing prophets, where we have their actual words, and where we are able to form more precise historical judgments. We shall see that what we have previously noticed occurs in a new form. Now, however, everything assumes even more serious dimensions. The prophetic message is directed against the entire covenant people, and threatens its very existence. Whilst it is not new that a threat arises from a violation of the law, the radical nature which this threat now assumes is quite new.

Von Rad argues that the function of the old law was merely to mark certain marginal situations in which a member of the covenant people was able to confess his God by his behaviour. With the prophets he finds something new, which he distinguishes from the old by the concept of a charismatic reinterpretation. It seems, however, that this concept is superfluous, and that we cannot differentiate the prophets from the old law in this way. What appears with the prophets is in no way a charismatic innovation, however much it goes beyond what was previously accepted. It is simply the emergence of a reality which lay dormant in the old law. The zealous God (Heb. *'el qanna'*) now appears as the guardian of the law which Israel has violated. The curse, with which the Law had already been enjoined at Shechem, and which had been mentioned as a real possibility when the covenant had been established, now turns fully against the transgressor of the divine will and judges him. The actual interpretation of the law is not new. The concern is still basically with the individual elements of the divine demand, which can already be seen in the Decalogue. What is new is the extent of the judgment which the transgression of the law entails. The law does not stop at the threat to an individual sinner. Neither is it confined to a threat to the existing royal dynasty, as with the prophets of the earlier period of the monarchy. It now encompasses the very existence of the entire covenant people, which is threatened by its covenant law. That this possibility lay dormant in the commandments is shown by the old narratives of the nation's sin during the desert wandering. According to Exodus xxxii. 7 ff. only the intercessory mediation of Moses saved the people from destruction by its God after their sin with the golden calf. Again according to Numbers xiv. 11 ff., in connection with Israel's disobedience over the story of the spies, the same thing occurs. In the time of the prophets there was no Moses to stand before the people. In this regard God angrily says to Jeremiah, 'Though Moses and Samuel stood before me, yet my heart would not turn toward this people. Send them out of my sight, and let them go" (Jer. xv. 1). Even a Moses or a Samuel would not be able to save the people now.

This extension in the range of the threatened judgment is undeniably connected with the contemporary situation of the prophets. They lived at a time when the very foundations of the states of their neighbouring Syro-Palestinian environment were shaking. The focus of the preceding centuries of the early period of the monarchy had been on the local wars of the neighbouring nations, which were no doubt painful enough, but which presented only a limited threat to Israel's existence. The subsequent radical danger to the existence of these smaller states from the growing power of Assyria revealed the severity of the threat which the divine judgment entailed for the existence of the covenant people of God.

Form-critical examination of the prophetic speeches has made clear that the special task of the prophets was the historical declaration of what was about to happen. The prophets were not men who arose with a new ethical sensitivity, which found its antithesis in the cult, and who then derived from the unconditional nature of the moral imperative the necessity of the divine judgment and the historical downfall of Israel, in the manner of a Kantian proposition. In Amos iv. 1 f. the prophet declared, 'Hear this word, you cows of Bashan, who are in the mountain of Samaria, who oppress the poor, who crush the needy, who say to their husbands, "Bring that we may drink!" The Lord Yahweh has sworn by his holiness that, behold, the days are coming upon you, when they shall take you away. . . .' We see clearly here that the specific word of God, which is introduced by a special formula as an oath of Yahweh, is the announcement of the carrying away into exile. Similarly in the first announcement of woe of Isaiah v, 'Woe to those who join house to house, who add field to field, until there is no more room, and you are made to dwell alone in the midst of the land. Yahweh of hosts has sworn in my hearing, "Surely many houses shall be desolate, large and beautiful houses, without inhabitant. For ten acres of vineyard shall yield but one bath, and a homer of seed shall yield but one ephah"' (Isa. v. 8 f.). Here too the word of God, which is introduced by a special oath formula, contains the announcement of God's future actions. Just as in war a messenger had to carry a report of the battle situation, so the prophetic messengers were conscious that they had been sent with a message describing the situation in which God was about to act in their day. This is clearly shown by the form of their sayings in the early classical prophets.

We must not, however, think that the prophets were simply interpreters of history, who kept their ears open to the historical situation, and adduced their message from it, and from the understanding which they had gained by reflecting upon it. History itself did not give the prophets their commission. It is their secret that, in spite of their close relationship to contemporary history, they were conscious of being the ambassadors of the God who stood above this history and who controlled it. He was the God who foretold the events of history, but who also retained the freedom to change a given announcement, and to make another. Behind the word of the prophet was not the river of history, rushing with invincible force, and by its rigid laws forcing its way on and breaking down all opposition. Behind their preaching stood the Lord of freedom, in whose hands all history remains a tool which can be wielded freely by him.

It is from this that the connection was made between the prophetic knowledge of the divine law, and their foretelling of historical events, but it would nevertheless be wrong to argue that the reference to the law, by which the coming judgment is justified, is nothing more than a personal and private reflection on the part of the prophet. When Amos points to the anti-social behaviour of the women who indirectly oppress the poor, then he shows thereby that he is bound by a revealed will of God. This is also true when Isaiah points to the buying up of property, which violates the old ordinance allocating the land by lot, and giving a share to every member of God's people, as the law of Jubilee in Leviticus xxv seeks to secure. The divine will revealed in the prophet's historical announcements is not a creation of the moment, but is in reality the divine will of the ancient law given to Israel by God. It is therefore no theological falsification when, at a later stage in its literary preservation, the reference to the divine law by which the message of judgment is justified, appears throughout as the word of God. This can be seen in the book of Jeremiah.[1] C. Westermann, in his study *Grundformen prophetischer Rede*,[2] is certainly correct in claiming that we cannot suppose that the rebuke and the threat were originally two quite separate forms of the prophetic preaching, as Gunkel argued.

From these general considerations we must now turn to the words of the individual classical prophets. Amos spoke against Northern Israel in the reign of Jeroboam II, about the middle of the eighth century, at a time when everything there appeared to be peaceful and secure. He declared, 'Hear this word, that Yahweh has spoken against you, O people of Israel, against the whole family which I brought up out of the land of Egypt: "You only have I known of all the families of the earth; therefore I will punish you for all your iniquities"' (Amos iii. 1 f.). No other statement, even in later prophecy, expresses more sharply that the entire judgment which threatens Israel is to be understood by nothing other than Israel's own relationship to its God. The word 'covenant' is not mentioned here. Instead there is a reference to 'election', or quite literally to God's 'knowing' his people. This is not a simple intellectual perception and insight, but rather a 'knowing', which in biblical usage means the choosing of the person concerned.[3] God has met and chosen his people, but this 'election', by which God has bound himself to his people is election by a zealous God, who does not fall in love blindly, but in whose love is contained the holy will

---

[1] H. WILDBERGER, *Jahwewort und prophetische Rede bei Jeremia*, Zürich, 1942.

[2] C. WESTERMANN, *Grundformen prophetischer Rede*, München, 1960.

[3] Cf. *TWzNT*, I, pp. 696–700.

expressed in his law. Thus whoever is 'known' by God stands neces-
sarily at the place where wrong becomes manifest as wrong.

Thus Amos speaks in his message again and again of the transgression
of Israel. Recent studies[1] have shown how Amos derives his accusations from quite explicit statements of the ancient law of God, which
we especially find in the Book of the Covenant. There it is stated that
the poor and the weak are not to be oppressed (Exod. xxii. 21 ff.,
Heb. 20 ff.); that the person who gives his garment as a pledge shall
have it restored by evening so that he might not be cold during the
night (Exod. xxii. 26 f., Heb. 25 f.); that interest is not to be taken on
loans (Exod. xxii. 25, Heb. 24). In Deuteronomy (Deut. xxv. 13–16)
and the Holiness Code (Lev. xix. 35 f.) we find the law prohibiting the
use of false measures and weights. All of these things are mentioned by
Amos in accusing the people of transgression. Alongside such concrete
violations of individual laws there are statements which point to a
breach of obedience to the more general guidance of God in history,
and to an insensibility towards true responsibility. 'Who sing idle songs
to the sound of the harp . . . who drink wine in bowls, and anoint
themselves with the finest oils, but are not grieved over the ruins of
Joseph' (Amos vi. 5 f.). Even the people's worship is a seduction, if it
deadens the real hearing of God's message.

Therefore the destruction must come. Amos describes it in different
ways; earthquake, future deportation and war. It is quite clear that he is
relatively unconcerned about the exact details in describing the coming
event. The important thing is that Israel should realize that God himself
comes in the judgment. Where Amos speaks of the coming day of
Yahweh we hear most fully the proclamation that it is the zealous
God himself who comes. He opposes all optimistic expectations of a
beautiful day of light, and insists that this day is darkness and not light,
gloomy and without brightness (Amos v. 18–20).

It is surprising that in between these strictures there stands at one
place an appeal of the prophet to the people to do good and to seek
Yahweh. The verses which express such an admonition are not to be
denied to the prophet, as some commentators suggest. Form-critical
examination shows that in them Amos does not employ the specific
style of prophetic speech, but the borrowed form of the priestly *torah*.[2]

[1] E. WURTHWEIN, 'Amos-studien', *ZAW* 62, 1950, especially pp. 40–52;
R. BACH, 'Gottesrecht und weltliches Recht in der Verkündigung des Propheten
Amos', *Festschrift Günther Dehn*, Neukirchen, 1957, pp. 23 ff.

[2] Cf. J. BEGRICH, 'Die priesterliche Tora'.

'Hate evil, and love good, and establish justice in the gate; it may be that Yahweh, the God of hosts, will be gracious to the remnant of Joseph' (Amos v. 15). The phrase 'it may be' preserves the sovereignty of God, who appears at this particular hour to be present only in a burning anger. In this 'perhaps' there is discernible once again the problem which arose in our consideration of the assertions of the law. The law was embedded in the reality of the covenant and of the gracious election of God. Perhaps, if the people found the way of repentance, grace might yet again be stronger than burning wrath in the judgment which preserves only a remnant of Joseph. Possibly this 'it may be' is the utmost that Amos dares to say, since it is not certain whether the closing words of the book of Amos, which speak affirmatively of a coming salvation (Amos ix. 11–13) really derive from the prophet himself.

The younger contemporary of Amos was Hosea. Unlike Amos, who was a Judean and was expelled from the Northern Kingdom as a foreigner, Hosea was a true member of North Israel. His preaching, which is preserved for us in a much more disturbed textual condition, is of interest to us in our concern with the problem of the law as an element of the covenant. In Hosea two things can be seen with great clarity. On the one hand there is the knowledge of God, who had become the God of Israel through a historical encounter, and who was to be known thereby. On the other hand there is the knowledge of the concrete unfolding of the law. In Hosea we can hear a very concrete argument about obedience towards the revealed law, 'Hear the word of Yahweh, O people of Israel; for Yahweh has a controversy with the inhabitants of the land. There is no faithfulness or kindness and no knowledge of God in the land; there is swearing, lying, killing, stealing, and committing adultery, they break all bounds and murder follows murder' (Hos. iv. 1 f.). Behind this accusation we can clearly hear a certain series of commandments, 'You shall not swear in falsehood; you shall not kill; you shall not commit adultery'. Hosea measures the people against the individual phrases of a composition similar to the Decalogue. In the preceding statement, 'There is no faithfulness or kindness and no knowledge of God in the land', there appears alongside these laws a deeper interpretation of the divine will, which not only expects obedience to the individual demands of the Decalogue, but also a right attitude towards God.

It can be seen in the preaching of Hosea that on the one side he measures the people against concrete commandments. The shedding of blood in the land, which was a daily occurrence in those revolutionary times, is held up to the people by the prophet. He begins with the bloodshed of Jehu, the ancestor of the current royal house, which took place at his usurpation of power (Hos. i. 4; cf. 2 Kings ix–x). The people have forgotten the first commandment, and instead tread the paths of primitive manticism and ask its 'tree and staff' for advice (Hos. iv. 12). The prophet strives above all for the second commandment, which was broken by the many images of God which led the people to forget their love for God. The prophet particularly attacks the golden bull image in Bethel, which changed in popular belief from being a pedestal for the invisible God throned upon it, to a representation of God himself (Hos. viii. 4–6; xiii. 2).

On the other hand behind these concrete accusations lies a deeper interpretation of God's law, which does not demand individual acts of obedience from men, but the obedience of the heart which expresses itself in every separate outward action. Thus Hosea demands faithfulness, kindness, and knowledge of God (Hos. iv. 1). In Amos the simple thought of gratitude for God's activity towards Israel stands in the foreground; Hosea goes deeper and considers the attitude of the heart towards God. The idea of the 'knowledge of God' is particularly important with him. This is not one-sidedly intellectual, a mere correct mental knowledge, and the avoidance of error. Knowledge of God is always also a recognition and a conscious relationship, which has a strong personal and intentional element. In this connection Hosea attacks with particular passion the priests who should have been the true guardians of the knowledge of God, and who have especially failed in this duty (Hos. iv. 4 ff.). They have allowed to pass unnoticed the very real exchange of Yahweh, the God of Israel, for the baals of Canaan. This was no longer the same threat which had occurred in Elijah's time, but was something much more dangerous. Whilst the worship of Yahweh remained outwardly correct, in reality he had come to be regarded as a nature deity like the Canaanite Baal. From him men sought the fertility of the soil and of marriage; he was worshipped with the forms of nature religion and with sacral prostitution, as men worshipped the baals. Yahweh became Baal. The name of one of David's warriors, which is recorded in 1 Chronicles xii. 5 as Bealiah (= Yahweh is Baal), demonstrates exactly this programmatic assertion. Thus, without knowing it, Israel had begun to misunderstand the very nature of its God, because the professional guardians of a true knowledge of him were asleep.

This loss of the true knowledge of God became clear to Hosea in a unique theology of history. In the beginning, when Israel was led by her God in the wilderness, everything went well for the people. Apostasy began with the entry into the land of Canaan. 'Like grapes in the wilderness, I found Israel. Like the first fruit on the fig tree, in its first season, I saw your fathers. But they came to Baal-peor, and consecrated themselves to Baal, and became detestable like the thing they loved' (Hos. ix. 10). Or again in a passage which goes even deeper and sees the danger of wealth and security for the heart of man, 'It was I who knew you in the wilderness, in the land of drought; but when they had fed to the full, they were filled, and their heart was lifted up; therefore they forgot me' (Hos. xiii. 5 f.). This theology of history should not be misunderstood, as though Hosea were speaking here of Israel's original goodness in the manner of a Rousseau, arguing that man is good, and only civilization makes him bad. Hosea xii speaks of the patriarch Jacob. The evil nature of Israel is already apparent in him. 'In the womb he took his brother by the heel (probably more correctly, 'He deceived his brother') and in his manhood he strove with God' (Hos. xii. 3, Heb. 4). The whole evil nature of Israel is already present in its ancestor, and now becomes manifest. Israel is unfaithful to God, and her heart is not wholly true to him. This also becomes apparent in its unstable political conduct, its alliances, and its seeking for help from those who are politically strong. The prophet himself, at the beginning of his activity, received from God the appalling command to marry, as a symbolic act, a 'wife of harlotry' (Hos. i. 2), i.e. probably a woman consecrated to the Baal-Yahweh cult through the impure sexual rites, and to have 'children of harlotry' by her. Thereby God's suffering on account of his adulterous people is made plain.

As in the preaching of Amos, there arises a curse out of the neglected law. Yahweh must become the enemy of his people. 'Therefore I am like a moth to Ephraim, and like dry rot to the house of Judah. . . . I will be like a lion to Ephraim, and like a young lion to the house of Judah. I, even I, will rend and go away, I will carry off, and none shall rescue (Hos. v. 12, 14). Through many of the prophet's words we hear, therefore, how he announced to the people judgment, wrath and the destruction of its political life. 'They shall return to the land of Egypt, and Assyria shall be their king, because they have refused to return to me. The sword shall rage against their cities, consume the bars of their gates, and devour them in their fortresses' (Hos. xi. 5 f.).

Here too we see that Hosea did not stop with the announcement of outward events. What takes place here is the curse arising out of the covenant, and falling upon the people. In Hosea too we hear the fearful consequence that the covenant itself will be shattered by this curse. The name given to his second child, a daughter, is already startling, Lo-ruhama (not pitied), Hosea i. 6. The mercy of God is at an end. The name of the third child, a son, goes even further than this, Lo-'ammi (not my people), Hosea i. 9. This means the end of the covenant relationship contained within the formula, 'You shall be my people, and I will be your God'. Through the name of his son, which will be spoken in the streets, the prophet dares to utter the final consequence; that Israel's violation of the divine law has brought forth the curses which were once declared in the ancient proclamation of the law. The totality of curses means that God regards his covenant as cancelled, and drives the people away from his presence, as he had once driven them away from Sinai.

It is striking that Hosea's message does not end with this, but takes a remarkable turn, as we have already seen briefly in the reference to chapter xi. We hear what sounds like an outburst of God's concealed emotion when we read, 'How can I give you up, O Ephraim! How can I hand you over, O Israel! How can I make you like Admah! How can I treat you like Zeboim! My heart recoils within me, my compassion grows warm and tender. I will not execute my fierce anger, I will not destroy Ephraim; for I am God and not man, the Holy One in your midst, and I will not come to destroy' (Hos. xi. 8 f.). This is a surprising outbreak of pity on the part of God. It is especially surprising that God justifies his outburst by asserting that he is holy. We are familiar with the holy one as the one who burns with anger against sin and avenges it. In God's identification of himself here as the holy one something deeper appears. The assertion of the Decalogue, combining the divine wrath and mercy, is here quite surprisingly broken through by the grace expressed in the Decalogue's preamble. The zealous God is throughout 'your God who brought you out of the house of bondage'. Where then is the holy zeal for the law?

We can see that the prophet himself faced this question. The mercy which appears here does not mean that God has set aside his zeal for the law. In Hosea ii. 14 ff. (Heb. 16 ff.) the prophet elaborates further on what God will do in the love which breaks through his judgment. 'Therefore, behold, I will allure her, and bring her into the wilderness, and speak tenderly to her. And there (or 'from there') I will give her her vineyards, and make the Valley of Achor a door of hope. And there she shall answer as in the days of her youth, as at the time when she came out of the land of Egypt' The question arises directly that if God begins again to deal with Israel, through judgment and deprivation, as he had once before done at the beginning of its history, will not everything which has happened simply repeat itself? We can see clearly that Hosea foresaw a future in which God would do even more. 'I will betroth you to me forever; I will betroth you to me in righteousness and justice, in steadfast love and in mercy. I will betroth you to me in faithfulness; and you shall know Yahweh' (Hos. ii. 19 f., Heb. 21 f.). In Israel the husband customarily paid a price at the betrothal which was the actual legal transfer of the bride to the man. Yahweh promises here to pay the price, and names righteousness and justice, steadfast love and mercy, and faithfulness, of which knowledge of God is the fruit. Hosea asserts by this that Yahweh himself will give to his people a new heart of righteousness and loyalty which they lack. Then they can again be called 'my people' (Hos. ii. 23, Heb. 25).

This carries the promise to the utmost limits. On the one hand we can see that Hosea has sought to understand God's new action in terms of a divine discipline. This can be found in chapter three, which reports a further symbolic action on the part of the prophet who disciplines his wife through a time of continence and privation. This signifies the period of privation which must come upon Israel through the judgment. On the other hand there is also the even stronger assertion of chapter two, according to which God himself accepts the cost of the new relationship, and renews the people, making them obedient.

We must now turn to Isaiah, who was contemporary with Hosea, but who prophesied in the Southern Kingdom. In his preaching the belief in the special election of the house of David and the city of David, Jerusalem, where Yahweh dwelt in the temple, plays an important role. In this temple Isaiah himself experienced his decisive encounter with God in which he was called to be a prophet. In his early preaching there seems to be a close relationship to Amos.[1] Like Amos he prophesies against the women of the capital city (Isa. iii. 16 ff.), and like him also he speaks of the coming day of Yahweh as a day of judgment (Isa. ii. 12 ff.). There is also a similarity to Amos when Isaiah, in the form of a priestly *torah*, contrasts the call to worship with a call to a true understanding of God's instruction. 'Your hands are full of blood. Wash yourselves; make yourselves clean; remove the evil of your doings from before my eyes; cease to do evil, learn to do good; seek justice,

[1] Cf. R. Fey, *Jesaia und Amos*, Neukirchen, 1963.

correct oppression; defend the fatherless, plead for the widow' (Isa. i. 15 ff.). Behind these positive demands we can recognize the injunctions of the ancient law of God. Like Amos Isaiah can utter a lament over his city. In Isaiah i. 21 ff. he calls Jerusalem a harlot, because it is sunken in injustice. This recalls the language of Hosea, as also does the lament of Isaiah i. 3, 'The ox knows its owner, and the ass its master's crib; but Israel does not know, my people does not understand.'

We could report in connection with Isaiah much that we have already said about Amos and Hosea. We shall limit ourselves here to stressing what is Isaiah's most distinctive emphasis. Isaiah vi tells how Isaiah, at the time of his call, encountered the holy God in the sanctuary, before whose presence he became conscious of his total worthlessness and uncleanness, being filled with great fear. This encounter determined his entire future preaching, and also the way in which he interpreted God's demand. To have no other God beside Yahweh meant for him the rejection of all human greatness. Wherever men boast, and rely upon their own strength, they do violence to the will of God. Thus, in rebuking the women of Jerusalem, Isaiah especially attacks their pride. The account of the coming day of Yahweh is a long description of judgment upon everything which exalts itself on earth. In the Syro-Ephraimitic war Isaiah confronted his king, who refused to submit his political actions to the judgment of God, and who rejected the help of the one who alone is mighty, the holy one in Israel. Isaiah contrasted this refusal with God's demand for faith (Isa. vii. 9). Faith means obedience towards the holy one of Israel. In this demand king Ahaz had failed, and again and again, in later years of political alliances, the people failed. Von Rad has argued that the key-word 'faith' probably derived from the terminology of the holy war, in which Israel was conscious that all its help came from God, because its wars were 'the wars of Yahweh'.[1] Faith stands at the centre of what Isaiah preached concerning politics, and constitutes the particular way in which he summarized the law of God. The people will be struck down by Yahweh in judgment because they do not observe this law. They refuse 'the waters of Shiloah that flow gently' (Isa. viii. 6), trusting instead in the power of human weapons. They do not want 'to be quiet and trust', but prefer to ride on horses, and to equip themselves with weapons (Isa. xxx. 15 f.). Here again we see the divine anger against those who disobey the law, interpreted by Isaiah in his own way in terms of faith. The law had become a threat to the people.

[1] G. VON RAD, *Der heilige Krieg im Alten Israel*, Zürich, 1951.

We also see in Isaiah, as in Hosea, that beyond this judgment Yahweh continues his historical purpose with his people. He is the holy one of Israel, who is determined to accomplish his will. In the lament over the harlot-city, Jerusalem, Isaiah speaks of a refining by fire in which everything that is unworthy will be removed, as smelting separates the dross from the pure metal (Isa. i. 25). Furthermore it is apparent that Isaiah lived in the theological tradition of Jerusalem, which was determined by the prophecy of Nathan. The ancient covenant of God with Israel took second place in Jerusalem to the promises made by God to the house of David, and to his city, and in particular to its temple. Thus Isaiah understands that through the whole judgment which will deeply humiliate Jerusalem, so that it speaks 'deep from the earth', and that her words shall come 'from low in the dust' (Isa. xxix. 4), God will again claim it as his city, and rescue it from all its enemies. Unlike Hosea, a deportation into the desert and into exile are not mentioned. Instead there appears in Isaiah mention of the new king, who, rightfully bears the name of 'son', and who is to receive wonderful royal titles. 'Of the increase of his government and of peace there will be no end, upon the throne of David, and over his kingdom, to establish it, and to uphold it with justice and with righteousness from this time forth and for evermore (Isa. ix. 7, Heb. 6). In this way God's law will finally be honoured through his righteous king.

The text of Isaiah's preaching is, in large measure, very different from that of Hosea. Nevertheless even here we learn from the prophet that God's demand, especially the demand for obedience in concrete political decisions, is a threat to the people. Isaiah i. 5–9, which is perhaps the last word of Isaiah, describes the total destruction of the land, under the judgment which the Assyrians have brought upon it at Yahweh's command. Isaiah ends in the deep confusion of this darkness, but beyond this darkness stands the promise of the holy one of Israel, who will remain faithful to his plan and his work (both of these are favourite terms of Isaiah). When Isaiah ix. 7 (Heb. 6) concludes with the promise, 'The zeal of Yahweh of hosts will do this', it expresses in a surprising way that all this is the direct action of a zealous God, so that it is Isaiah's way of referring to the '*el qanna*'.

6. The Prophets of the Seventh and Sixth Centuries

IN the preaching of the prophets of the eighth century a terrifying occurrence had taken place. For a long time Israel had lived with its divine law. When this law was proclaimed at the great festivals, Israel was repeatedly made conscious that it was the people of Yahweh. Now, however, men had appeared who pointed back to this law, and in God's name declared that Israel had ceased to be Yahweh's people. The curse of the law, which had seemed to stand merely as a protection for it, had turned threateningly against the people, and had separated them from God, delivering them to judgment and destruction. The prophets announced that only a new mighty act of God would enable Israel once again, through judgment and privation, to become God's people.

Then history began to speak. The ten tribes of Northern Israel disappeared from the political map, and only the small southern state was left, with Jerusalem as its capital, and a successor of David as its king. For half a century the prophetic word was silent in this small land during the evil time of Manasseh. Then once again God spoke through the word of the prophets. They delivered their message during the last turbulent decades in which disaster began to descend upon the small Southern Kingdom, continuing into the darkness of the Babylonian exile. Jeremiah, Ezekiel and Deutero-Isaiah all appeared during these years.

Jeremiah was called to be a prophet during the early years of king Josiah, at a time when the strong arm of Assyrian rule began to weaken, and when independent life could awaken again in the land. There is some similarity to the brighter years of the Northern Kingdom under Jeroboam II, when Amos had appeared. It is striking how little sense of relief is found, even in Jeremiah, at this possibility of a greater measure of freedom, which shows that the prophets did not simply derive their message from the historical situation which they found. On the contrary we find in Jeremiah the whole message of God's judgment announced again.[1] His preaching especially recalls that of Hosea. The message of judgment, proclaimed in his early oracles, has its own

[1] For more complete information about the problems of Jeremiah's early preaching see H. H. ROWLEY, 'The Early Prophecies of Jeremiah in their Setting', *BJRL* 45, 1962, pp. 198–234, and cf. also the literature cited there.

special form. He speaks of an irresistible enemy swarming out from the North. The question has frequently been raised whether this points to the experience of marauding peoples, such as the Scythians. The view of Israel's history, however, which conceives of an initial period of loving union with its God, is reminiscent of Hosea. 'I remember the devotion of your youth, your love as a bride, how you followed me in the wilderness, in a land not sown. Israel was holy to Yahweh, the first fruits of his harvest. All who ate of it became guilty; evil came upon them, says Yahweh' (Jer. ii. 2 f.). Israel broke off this union, when it entered into the rich land of Canaan. Here it became involved in the disloyalty of 'baalizing' its faith. Hosea's preaching is here echoed by Jeremiah.

The reference to the breaking of individual commandments is, however, less prominent in the words of Jeremiah. The people's lack of knowledge, their forgetfulness of God, their inner dishonesty, are the things which distress him. Like Hosea he can describe in impressive prayers of popular lamentation, which he quotes, days of penitence, which the people observe in a period of drought (Jer. iii. 21 ff.; xiv. 1 ff.). These, however, lead to no genuine repentance, The word 'lie' plays a noticeably prominent role in the preaching of Jeremiah. On all sides he discovers lies among the people. He does not mean this in the narrow sense of breaking one of the Ten Commandments, which demands truthful testimony in lawsuits, but in a much broader and deeper sense of a sinful attitude of the people towards God.

In 2 Kings xxii–xxiii we read of the great reform which king Josiah carried through in the eighteenth year of his reign, and in which the book of Deuteronomy must have played some part. It is a question, which has never been satisfactorily answered, whether Jeremiah made any reference to this reform. Probably he remained silent during this time, for he was certainly not a propagandist for it. The prophet was no teacher of law, and such was not his office. Yet neither did Jeremiah speak against the reform. In the narrative sections of his book we can see clearly that after the reform he frequently found understanding and even protection in dangerous situations among the circles of men, who had participated in the reform, or among the sons of such men.[1] Does this silence of the prophet during the period of reform mean that God was waiting, and pausing to see whether the people would really return to seek his will?

Josiah fell in battle against the Egyptian army, when it was moving

---

[1] Cf. for instance Jer. xxvi. 24; xxxvi. 25.

northwards under Pharaoh Necho. In place of Jehoahaz, who had been chosen by the people and who obviously intended to continue the political policy of his father Josiah, the Egyptian king appointed another of Josiah's sons, Jehoiakim, as ruler. The so-called temple speech of Jeremiah belongs to the beginning of this king's reign. Jeremiah xxvi reports the dramatic events occasioned by the prophet's preaching. Its text is given in Jeremiah vii. 1–15 with greater detail, where its formulation has been coloured by Deuteronomistic editorial work. In it Jeremiah threatened the destruction of the temple. The reason for this judgment is the false sense of security with which the people run to the temple, so recently reformed by Josiah, and say, 'The temple of Yahweh, the temple of Yahweh, the temple of Yahweh is here'. They think that they will be protected here from all danger. Jeremiah asks, 'Will you steal, murder, commit adultery, swear falsely, burn incense to Baal, and go after other gods that you have not known, and then come and stand before me in this house, which is called by my name, and say, "We are delivered"—only to go on doing all these abominations?' As in Hosea iv. 2 we see here the confrontation of the people with a series of apodictic laws similar to those of the Decalogue. With this law the prophet lays bare the sin of the people who believe themselves secure in the house of their God.

In another way the confrontation with a very concretely formulated law appears in a prophecy which Jeremiah uttered against king Jehoiakim himself. In spite of the fact that the land had just been forced to pay a heavy tribute, the king believed that he could be a great builder like Solomon. In this he disregarded the fundamental ordinances of God. Both in Deuteronomy and the Holiness Code the law is stated that the day-labourer is to be paid his wage before sunset, because he needs it (Lev. xix. 13; Deut. xxiv. 14 f.). Jeremiah has to say to Jehoiakim. 'Woe to him who builds his house by unrighteousness, and his upper rooms by injustice; who makes his neighbour serve him for nothing, and does not give him his wages' (Jer. xxii. 13).

The prophet holds up God's law to the person who is breaking it. In another passage, which cannot be precisely dated, we see the prophet in conflict with the people who, at the opposite extreme, make their boast in the law of Yahweh. Possibly we can see in this an indirect consequence of the Deuteronomic reform. In this dispute the prophet says, 'How can you say, "We are wise, and the law (*torah*) of Yahweh is with us'? But behold the false pen of the scribes has made it into a lie. The wise men shall be put to shame, they shall be dismayed and taken;

lo, they have rejected the word of Yahweh, and what wisdom is in them?' (Jer. viii. 8 f.). Here the appeal to the *torah*, which is claimed by a special group as its private possession and wisdom, rebounds against the living word of the prophet. The divine will can be falsified in the law when it hardens into dead propositions, and no longer derives from the understanding of an attitude to God. The prophet has this to say to the teachers of *torah*, with the full authority of the divine word.

Jehoiakim's politics left an evil legacy for his people. As a friend of Egypt he had thought to build a barrier across the course of history, which handed over the Assyrian empire in Syria and Palestine as a legacy to the Neo-Babylonian king, Nebuchadnezzar. His son Jehoiachin had to bear the consequences of his father's political actions immediately after his accession to the throne. He was deported to the east along with large numbers of the people. During the reign of his successor, Zedekiah, Jeremiah proclaimed, at God's command, that the people would have to bear the yoke of Babylonian rule. Only in the acceptance of this judgment of God was there still hope for the future of the people. The prophet, however, had to undergo fierce opposition even from groups of prophets among the people. The last days of Jerusalem, before the city and temple went up in flames, were for him a continual battle (Jer. xxxvii ff.). After the city had fallen he was carried to Egypt by a group of refugees, where we lose all trace of him. Right to the last he encountered the inability of his people to hear the law of God. On one occasion, in a sombre word of lamentation, he decried the corruption of the people, 'Can the Ethiopian change his skin or the leopard his spots? Then also you can do good who are accustomed to do evil' (Jer. xiii. 23).

A word in the book of Jeremiah, which may originally have been spoken in a different context, and which betrays the Deuteronomistic editorial activity, shows that with Jeremiah, and those who preserved his message, the idea had clearly emerged that Israel's fate was decided by its attitude to the law. Israel's only hope lay in the promise of God to change this. Jeremiah xxxi. 31 ff. says, 'Behold, the days are coming says Yahweh, when I will make a new covenant with the house of Israel and the house of Judah, not like the covenant which I made with their fathers when I took them by the hand to bring them out of the land of Egypt, my covenant which they broke, though I was their husband, says Yahweh. But this is the covenant which I will make with the house of Israel after those days, says Yahweh: I will put my law within them, and I will write it upon their hearts; and I will be their

God, and they shall be my people. And no longer shall each man teach his neighbour and each his brother, saying, "Know Yahweh", for they shall all know me, from the least of them to the greatest, says Yahweh; for I will forgive their iniquity, and I will remember their sin no more.' As in Hosea it is established here that Israel's fundamental need is for the knowledge of God. The insight here, however, goes beyond Hosea, and asserts that a true knowledge of God is only possible where a new attitude to the law exists. This must no longer speak to man from outside, as in the covenant festival, or in a private instruction given by others. It must live in the heart of every individual. The further realization that this new understanding can only be attained by a new beginning, which goes behind the Sinai covenant, is a radical innovation. The prophet announces here the end of the Mosaic covenant, which had brought death to Israel for its disobedience.

These insights were further developed and intensified in the words of the prophet Ezekiel.[1] He was among the exiles deported with Jehoiachin. His preaching and thought were at many points strongly influenced by Jeremiah, and Ezekiel begins with the position that the judgment has taken place. In his preaching of judgment Ezekiel is the most sombre of all the prophets. The statement of Joshua to the assembly of Israel at Shechem, 'You cannot serve Yahweh; for he is a holy God; he is a jealous God; he will not forgive your transgressions or your sins . . . he will turn and do you harm, and consume you' (Jos. xxiv. 19 f.) receives in Ezekiel an uncompromising interpretation. The holy wrath of God against those who break his law, the inability of the people to keep this law, and the resultant death which threatens the people, indeed the whole threatening aspect of the law, is fully expressed in Ezekiel.

We find in this prophet the various ways in which the law confronts the people. Sometimes the people are shown their disobedience to individual laws in a kind of catalogue held up before them. Thus Ezekiel xxii speaks of Jerusalem as the city of blood, 'Behold, the princes of Israel in you, everyone according to his power, have been bent on shedding blood. Father and mother are treated with contempt in you; the sojourner suffers extortion in your midst; the fatherless and the widow are wronged in you. You have despised my holy things, and profaned my sabbaths. . . . In you men take bribes to shed blood; you take interest and increase and make gain of your neighbours by

[1] With regard to details see my exegesis in *Biblischer Kommentar* 13, Neukirchen, 1955–.

extortion; and you have forgotten me, says the Lord Yahweh' (Ezek. xxii. 6–12). The prophet runs down the list of commandments and, recounting law by law, establishes the guilt of the city Jerusalem, which can therefore not escape the full judgment. 'I will scatter you among the nations and disperse you through the countries.'

Beside this we find long sketches of history which frequently, with almost unbearable harshness, establish that evil is the original nature of this people. It is uncovered by Yahweh's providential guidance in history. Thus Ezekiel xvi describes the history of Jerusalem as that of a young girl. She comes from heathen parents. Her father was an Amorite and her mother a Hittite, who abandoned her as a child. Yahweh took her up from the field and saved her life, dressing her in fine clothes, and finally taking her as his wife. The girl, however, repaid all this with ingratitude and played the harlot with other men. What Hosea and Jeremiah had preached reappears here greatly intensified. In a slightly different simile, which was, however, already anticipated in Jeremiah iii, Ezekiel xxiii tells of two women, who symbolize the two divided kingdoms of Israel. They came out of Egypt, thus reflecting the old credo–like historical summaries. Already in Egypt, however, they became immoral, and the entire subsequent history of these two wives of Yahweh stands under this sign. The thought here is especially focussed on the foreign political intrigues and treaties of the two kingdoms. In Ezekiel xx the story of Israel's sin is again related, this time without any symbolic imagery. The election of Israel in Egypt, the giving of the law, the exodus and the wandering in the wilderness are all narrated in plain language. It is the great credal history of Israel, but from the very beginning everything is set in the sombre light of a history of sin and of the continual violation of Yahweh's law. Thus Yahweh finally decides, already during the people's stay in the desert, to send them into exile.

In this regard there appears a quite unique statement about Yahweh's law, which is otherwise always understood as Yahweh's own gift, and as a divinely given help for living. We read in Ezekiel xx. 11, 13, 21 of 'ordinances, by whose observance man shall live', and Ezekiel xxxiii. 15 refers to 'statutes of life'. Ezekiel xx. 25 f., however, in referring to the increasing punishment of Yahweh, says, 'I gave them statutes that were not good and ordinances by which they could not have life; and I defiled them through their gifts in making them offer by fire all their first-born, that I might horrify them'. The reference is to the demand for the first-born which is mentioned in the Book of the Covenant

(Exod. xxii. 29, Heb. 28). Ezekiel understands it as a harmful demand of God's anger which leads the people to commit the sin of burning their children.[1] This goes far beyond the statement of Jeremiah viii, 8 f. in which the lying pen of the scribes has turned the *torah* into a lie. Here the law becomes a means through which God himself causes Israel's sin to be magnified. What is said here concerning a single commandment occurs later in Paul in an even deeper perspective in the light of Jesus Christ as a statement about the law as a whole.

Thus before the law of God Israel appears as the 'house of rebellion' (Heb. *beth meri*), which has been radically corrupted by sin. Ezekiel xv derives the knowledge of the complete worthlessness of the people from the familiar picture of the vine, which occurs frequently in religious language (Ps. lxxx. 8 ff., Heb. 9 ff.). Just as its wood can only be used for burning, so also Jerusalem is by its nature predestined for the fire of judgment. This approaches the ideas of predestination and of original sin.

Ezekiel however, proclaims a future for the people beyond the judgment, which found its historical fulfilment in 587 with the burning of Jerusalem and the destruction of the temple. In this Ezekiel is the heir of the preaching of the earlier prophets, who had declared of God that his love, as the opening of the Decalogue declared it, would finally overcome the holy wrath, which is expressed in the commandment prohibiting idolatry. We must notice, however, how the prophet speaks of this event. Ezekiel xxxvii. 1–14 describes the impressive vision of the awakening of dead bones, which lay completely dried out in a field, and which received new life through the word of God proclaimed to them. This event depicts symbolically God's plan for his people. 'I will put my spirit within you, and you shall live, and I will place you in your own land; then you shall know that I, Yahweh, have spoken, and I have done it, says Yahweh.' The new event, which is about to take place for God's people according to his promise, can only be described in the category of an awakening of the dead. The entire former history of the people, with its ordinances and its covenant, was dead, but God, who had promised his love to Israel, lives. As the creator, who can awaken the dead to life through a new act of creation, he would deal afresh with his people for the sake of his promise. The awakening of dead bones is reminiscent of Genesis ii.

[1] He has in mind here the literal interpretation of the commandment thus employed, beginning with the time of Ahaz (2 Kings xvi. 3) and Manasseh (2 Kings xxi. 6); cf. also Mic. vi. 7.

Ezekiel emphasizes very firmly that this new event is not founded on any possibilities latent within the people. They are dead on account of their sin, and only God's faithfulness to himself and his zeal for the honour of his name can effect this new life. 'Son of man, when the house of Israel dwelt in their own land, they defiled it by their ways and their doings. . . . So I poured out my wrath upon them. . . . I scattered them among the nations, and they were dispersed through the countries. . . . But when they came to the nations, wherever they came, they profaned my holy name, in that men said of them, "These are the people of Yahweh, and yet they had to go out of his land". . . . Therefore say to the house of Israel, Thus says the Lord Yahweh: It is not for your sake, O house of Israel, that I am about to act, but for the sake of my holy name, which you have profaned among the nations to which you came. And I will vindicate the holiness of my great name, which has been profaned among the nations, and which you have profaned among them; and the nations will know, that I am Yahweh, says the Lord Yahweh, when through you I vindicate my holiness before their eyes' (Ezek. xxxvi. 16 ff.). Ezekiel is the prophet of the majesty of God, but this majesty cannot endure that God's name should be blasphemed among the nations when they scoff that God has not been able to carry to a conclusion the election of his people. Now the people are again lost and sold into slavery as they had once before been in Egypt.

At this point we may raise the question whether the majesty of this God, the *'el qanna'*, who is jealously concerned for his law, does not demand his merciless opposition against all transgression of his law. Is it then possible for Israel, which has been marked by sin and has thereby stained God's name, to glorify his honour in the world? The preaching of Ezekiel answers this question. In Ezekiel xx. 32 ff. we have an answer to an expression of despair on the part of those in exile.[1] First it is said that God will stand by his promise given at the exodus from Egypt. He will lead out the people from their exile among the nations in a new exodus. 'With a mighty hand and an outstretched arm, and with wrath poured out, I will be king over you. I will bring you out from the peoples. . . .' This clearly echoes the language used of the first exodus. God will again lead his people through the desert. As he had once led Israel's ancestors 'in the wilderness of the land of Egypt', so he will now lead them from the nations 'into the wilderness of the

---

[1] Ezek. xx. 32 provides the context of the following verses, and it shows the danger of an inner paralysis on the part of the exiles, and their assimilation to the pagan environment.

peoples'. This phrase, which is quoted in the writings from Qumran, is not intended geographically, but is rather an antitype. The question arises immediately as to what will happen after this. In the old narrative of the exodus there followed the account of the making of the covenant on Mount Sinai, at which God gave his commandments to his people and thereby secured the majesty of his covenant. Yet it was the law of this very covenant which had been the downfall of Israel. Ezekiel continues further, 'I will bring you into the wilderness of the peoples, and there I will enter into judgment with you face to face. . . . I will make you pass under the rod, and I will let you go in by number. I will purge out the rebels from among you, and those who transgress against me; I will bring them out of the land where they sojourn, but they shall not enter the land of Israel' (Ezek. xx. 35 ff.).

This no longer speaks of a covenant like that of Mount Sinai, in which God's demand was proclaimed, but is a judgment of separation. As the shepherd separates the sheep under his staff, so God will separate the sinners in judgment in order that they might not return to the land. Jesus used this picture in the parable of the last judgment in Matthew xxv. Some verses later we are told by Ezekiel that in the land God will establish his sanctuary, 'For on my holy mountain, the mountain height of Israel, says the Lord Yahweh, there all the house of Israel, all of them, shall serve me in the land; there I will accept them, and there I will require your contributions and the choicest of your gifts, with all your sacred offerings' (Ezek. xx. 40). Later Ezekiel says that the people will remember their former evil ways, and bow down humbly before their God.

We raised the question whether God's majesty demands his merciless opposition to all evil and impurity. The judgment, which God will execute upon the people in the wilderness, at the threshhold of their return, expresses this opposition. Further we see how the prophet answers the question that has been raised in two ways, when he comes to consider Israel's future life in the land. On the one hand he looks to the people as a whole, and asserts that its new life will be based on the new sanctuary, which will stand on the high mountains of Israel, and from which purity will go out into the land. In Ezekiel xl ff. the prophet, and probably a group of his disciples, developed this vision of a new temple, almost in the form of a programme for the future. This sanctuary will be separated from all impurity, and in it pure worshippers will offer pure worship to Yahweh. In this vision the prophet sees the miracle of a new temple, which would not be built by human hands, but by God himself. In connection with it Ezekiel xlvii. 1 ff. speaks of a miraculous river, which originates in the temple, and from which healing will spread throughout the land. Even the Dead Sea, the geographical enigma of the Holy Land, will be healed by it.

On the other hand the prophet speaks to individual members of the people. In a manner strongly reminiscent of Jeremiah, he affirms that God will give a new nature to each individual, 'I will sprinkle clean water upon you, and you shall be clean from all your uncleannesses, and from all your idols I will cleanse you. A new heart I will give you, and a new spirit I will put within you; and I will take out of your flesh the heart of stone and give you a heart of flesh. And I will put my spirit within you, and cause you to walk in my statutes and be careful to observe my ordinances' (Ezek. xxxvi. 25 ff.). Hosea had spoken of the price paid by God for his bride, and through which he himself brought her new life. Jeremiah xxxi spoke of the new covenant in which the law would be written on the hearts of the people. Ezekiel speaks of the new obedience towards God's law which, as the gift of God, would be effected by the gift of God's own spirit. Thus the majesty of God, which is that of *'el qanna'* who is jealous for obedience to his law, will receive honour from a people in whose hearts God has himself written obedience.

There is still one feature lacking in the picture of Ezekiel, when we ask about the significance of the law in his preaching. Ezekiel lived among the exiles, and we can understand that he met many different attitudes among these people. Some despaired, saying, 'Our transgressions and our sins are upon us, and we waste away because of them; how then can we live'? (Ezek. xxxiii. 10). On the other hand the cynical attitude of those who remained in Palestine obviously penetrated through to the exiles. They said, 'The fathers have eaten sour grapes, and the children's teeth are set on edge' (Ezek. xviii. 2). They scoffed that there was no such thing as a divine righteousness. In both passages we see how the prophet spoke to these people, who both equally felt themselves subjected to an unalterable fate. It is often said that Ezekiel preached a doctrine of individual retribution. This, however, does not truly represent the prophet's intention. He endeavoured rather to encourage these people who were oppressed by their fate, by assuring them that there was a future, even personally for each of them. Their past guilt need not oppress their present life. They must therefore return to God, who does not will the death of the sinner, but rather that he may live (Ezek. xviii. 23, 32; xxxiii. 11). In answer to the

question of what Israel must do in the present, Ezekiel simply points
to the old ordinances of the law. In Ezekiel xviii. 5 ff. there appear in
succession descriptions of a righteous man, the sinful son of a righteous
man and the righteous son of a sinful man. It is probable that Ezekiel is
using here an old form, derived from the temple cult, which was related
to a series of apodictic laws, and which described on this basis the
commandments of the law under which a man stands. Psalm xv. 2–4
and Isaiah xxxiii. 14 ff. show that such formulations were used at the
temple gates in order to examine the life of the pilgrim who wished to
enter the sanctuary. Whoever passed the examination was assured by
the priest that he was considered righteous, and that he would share
the 'life' which was given at the sanctuary through the priestly blessing.
With Ezekiel, who was among the exiles, all this took on a totally
different role. We hear in his words the same answer which Jesus gave
to the rich young ruler who asked, 'Teacher, what good deed must I
do to have eternal life?' To this Jesus replied, 'If you would enter life,
keep the commandments' (Matt. xix. 16 f.).[1] Ezekiel faced those who
were discouraged and cynical, who both no longer believed in a future,
yet to whom the message of the prophets had given the great promise
of an imminent new beginning with God. In looking at their present
dilemma the prophet says, 'Repent, keep the commandments'. This is
the will of God in which is the promise of life. We find in Ezekiel,
however, no answer to the question how this obedience, and the great
hope of the coming creative act of God, were related. Nevertheless
we have very clearly the assurance that there was a future, and in this
future God's law over them remained holy, righteous and good
(cf. Rom. vii. 12).

The message of Ezekiel cannot be overestimated in its importance
for the subsequent history of Israel. The great themes of the following
period were anticipated by him. In the later period of the exile yet
another prophet arose among the exiles, whose words are preserved in
Isaiah xl–lv, and who is usually referred to as Deutero-Isaiah. In his
whole manner of speaking he is a very different prophet from Ezekiel.
He comes from the world of the Psalms, the world of praises sung to
God. Nevetheless he takes up a theme which is already found in
Ezekiel, that of the new exodus. His words are nothing but one great
jubilation over this immediately impending exodus from Babylon. In
glowing colours he describes the glory of this exodus from the house

[1] Cf. my article 'Die Frage des Reichen nach dem ewigen Leben', *Ev.Th.* 19,
1959, pp. 90–97; reprinted in *Gottes Offenbarung*, pp. 316–24.

of bondage, which will be more glorious than the exodus from Egypt. Yahweh himself leads the procession through the desert, which is itself transformed by this event. In Zion the messengers, filled with joy, cry out when they see the approaching procession. In great splendour the ruins of Jerusalem will again be built.

This impressive evangelist saw in the figure of the Persian king, Cyrus, quite explicitly the man through whom God would effect the great return home. When we examine his preaching about the law, and the divine justice proclaimed in the covenant, his answer is remarkably vague. He knows of the tragic history of disobedience from which Israel comes. 'Yet you did not call upon me, O Jacob. . . . You have not bought me sweet cane with money, or satisfied me with the fat of your sacrifices. But you have burdened me with your sins, you have wearied me with your iniquities' (Isa. xliii. 22 f.). Just as Ezekiel he knows that it is only by the free grace of God that deliverance comes. 'I, I am he who blots out your transgressions for my own sake, and I will not remember your sins. Put me in remembrance, let us argue together; set forth your case, that you may be proved right. Your first father sinned and your mediators transgressed against me' (Isa. xliii. 25). As already in Hosea, and also in Jeremiah, there is a reference here to the sin of the ancestor Jacob, in which the whole iniquity of all his descendants was signified. Elsewhere the prophet addressed his people as blind and deaf.

When, however, we ask what kind of law will be given to the liberated people, and what significance this law will have in the impending bright future, then we find only a few incidental remarks. Isaiah xliv. 22 says, 'I have swept away your transgressions like a cloud. and your sins like mist; return to me, for I have redeemed you', Isaiah lv. 6 f. makes the appeal, 'Seek Yahweh, while he may be found. call upon him while he is near; let the wicked forsake his way, and the unrighteous man his thoughts; let him return to Yahweh, that he may have mercy on him, and to our God, for he will abundantly pardon.' In both cases we have only the exhortation to return to God already familiar to us from Ezekiel and the earlier prophets. Nowhere in Deutero-Isaiah do we find a more specific demand in terms of particular laws.

With this goes a further feature. The prophet proclaims the new exodus with great joy, and describes the journey through the wilderness. In this many details of the earlier narrative of the exodus and the desert wandering reappear: the destruction of the Egyptians in the sea, the miraculous supply of food in the wilderness, the drinking of water from the rock and the accompanying presence of God. Thus we are prompted to ask, as in Ezekiel xx, whether the prophet envisaged a new Sinai-event. Does he not describe an encounter with God, and the proclamation of a new covenant and law? In fact nothing of this sort is found. Everything focuses rather on Mount Zion, newly populated, and newly rebuilt in splendour, in which God himself will be king. A new covenant is mentioned, but it is striking that in both places where this occurs,[1] there is no reference to Moses as the lawgiver. In Isaiah liv. 9 f., we find, 'For this is like the days of Noah to me: as I swore that the waters of Noah should no more go over the earth, so I have sworn that I will not be angry with you and will not rebuke you'. The primeval history of Genesis recounts that God had promised unconditionally to Noah that such a flood would never again come upon the earth. In Isaiah lv. 3 ff. we read, 'Incline your ear, and come to me; hear, that your soul may live; and I will make with you an everlasting covenant, my steadfast, sure love for David. Behold, I made him a witness to the peoples, a leader and commander for the peoples. Behold, you shall call nations that you know not, and nations that knew you not shall run to you, because of Yahweh your God, and of the Holy One of Israel, for he has glorified you.' This is a reference to the covenant with David. It is a feature of this covenant that God gives it freely, and that it is not connected with a proclamation of law. Just as David was a witness to the magnificent goodness of God, so the delivered Israel will now be God's witness before the eyes of the nations, and will proclaim his redemptive grace.[2]

Thus Deutero-Isaiah preached very forcefully the advent of the mighty acts of Yahweh's grace towards his people, which were about to take place. He was commissioned to declare that God would demonstrate in the near future, and in a new way, the truth contained in the preamble of the Decalogue. Yaweh is 'your God, who brought you out of the house of bondage'.

Does this mean that Moses is in fact completely absent from the preaching of Deutero-Isaiah? This question raises immediately the problem of the servant songs, the unique character of which was first

---

[1] For Is. xlii. 6 and xlix. 8 see footnote 1 below page 90.

[2] In Deutero-Isaiah's preaching David is considered under the category of a 'witness', just as is Israel itself (Isa. xliii. 10, 12). The specific expectation of a Davidic messiah plays no part here, and the title of 'anointed one' is bestowed upon Cyrus (Isa. xlv. 1).

brought to light by B. Duhm.[1] There are in Isaiah xl–lv a series of passages, or songs, distributed at intervals throughout the book, which speak of a servant of Yahweh, who has a special function to fulfil. In these songs, the number of which remains disputed, it is clear that the servant, who also has a task to accomplish for the nations outside Israel, is led into suffering. The last great song, Isaiah lii. 13–liii. 12, which differs in its language more sharply from the rest of Deutero-Isaiah, shows a suffering unto death, over which God places a great promise. The closest parallels to these songs are the so-called confessions of Jeremiah, in which the increasingly severe suffering of the prophet Jeremiah is described. These psalm-like compositions are distributed throughout the book of Jeremiah, with the same arbitrariness as the servant songs appear in Deutero-Isaiah. Here too the last of these passages, in which Jeremiah curses his own life, leads into the lowest depths of despair.

According to Isaiah xlix. 5 f. the servant receives at first from God the task, 'to bring Jacob back to him', and 'to raise up the tribes of Jacob and to restore the preserved of Israel'. It is impossible, therefore, to assume that the servant is simply Israel itself, even though in Isaiah xlix. 3 'Israel' does appear as a mysterious gloss. On the other hand the description of the servant's task, who, according to Isaiah xlii. 3, will not break the bruised reed or extinguish a dimly burning wick, is strikingly similar to the task which the unknown prophet himself fulfils in his message. He announces salvation to the bruised reed, and to the dimly burning wick of Israel, and he gathers the tribes for their return. Do we not find in this the features of a new Moses? Does the prophet then not understand his office as that of a new Moses? We cannot dismiss such ideas lightly.[2] There is, however, a surprising feature. The first song mentions a proclamation of 'justice' and 'law' (Isa. xlii. 3 f.), but in the subsequent songs a totally different picture of the servant of God emerges. What is outlined in the confessions of Jeremiah reaches here its utmost depths. The task of the servant ultimately consists in vicariously bearing the guilt of others. An unidentified group in Isaiah liii. 1–11a confesses this very fact when they express

[1] For recent studies of the servant songs cf. C. R. NORTH, *The Suffering Servant in Deutero-Isaiah*, Oxford, 1948, 2nd ed. 1956; H. H. ROWLEY, 'The Servant of the Lord in the Light of Three Decades of Criticism', *The Servant of the Lord and Other Essays on the Old Testament*, London, 1952, and W. ZIMMERLI and J. JEREMIAS, *The Servant of God* (SBT 20), London, 1957.

[2] Cf. the study of A. BENTZEN, *King and Messiah*, London, 1953.

their complete amazement at the mysterious suffering of the servant. 'We esteemed him stricken, smitten by God, and afflicted. But he was wounded for our transgressions, he was bruised for our iniquities; upon him was the chastisement that made us whole, and with his stripes we are healed. All we like sheep have gone astray; we have turned every one to his own way; and Yahweh has laid on him the iniquity of us all' (Isa. liii. 4 ff.). If we regard this as the task of Moses, then in place of a lawgiver we have one who suffers vicariously.[1] Even if we do not think directly of Moses, it is in any case evident that at the centre of the message of the liberation, which God is about to give to his people, there stands one who bears the guilt of others by his suffering, and thus makes this liberation possible.

Prophecy did not go beyond the message of Ezekiel and Deutero-Isaiah. Those prophets who came after the exile merely developed the earlier prophetic message in a number of ways. Trito-Isaiah (Isa. lvi–lxvi), especially in Isaiah lx–lxii, shows how prophecy treasured the great promises of the earlier prophets,[2] whilst Haggai and Zechariah point to the coming age of salvation and the advent of the anointed one. In Malachi the prophet takes up the role of preaching judgment and of warning the people, in the manner of the earlier classical prophets. We need not, however, pursue this investigation further.

We must, in closing, consider briefly once again the law of the Priestly Document, to which Wellhausen ascribed a post-exilic date. Contrary to Wellhausen's view we can now see more clearly that much ancient material has been reworked in this later part of the Pentateuch. Wellhausen, however, was right in arguing that it owes its own distinctive theological form to the post-exilic age. We shall show this by a point which leads us again into the central problem of these lectures.

We began with the problem of the law, and we saw that in the earliest period this was completely embedded in the proclamation of the covenant between Yahweh and Israel. This took place in regular cultic celebrations in which the law was read out, as we find mentioned in Deuteronomy xxxi. 10 f. The older narratives of the Sinai event in Exodus xix, xx, xxiv are governed by this fact. In the Priestly Document, however, we have the striking fact that it no longer mentions

---

[1] The usual designation of berit 'am for the servant in Isa. xlii. 6 and xlix. 8 could possibly be understood thus.

[2] For the relationship of Deutero-Isaiah to Trito-Isaiah see my remarks in 'Zur Sprache Tritojesaias', Festschrift Ludwig Köhler, Zürich, 1950, pp. 62–71, reprinted in Gottes Offenbarung, pp. 217–33.

a covenant on Mount Sinai.[1] Wellhausen wanted to designate the Priestly Document as Q (*liber quattuor foederum*) because he regarded it as built upon four covenants. In fact, however, it only mentions two: the covenant with Noah and the covenant with Abraham. The Priestly Document regards the events of the age of Moses as the fulfilment of the promise made to Abraham, so that from the theological viewpoint it belongs with the Abraham covenant. In the account of the promise to Abraham contained in the Priestly Document Yahweh promises to Abraham, 'And I will establish my covenant between me and you and your descendants after you throughout their generations for an ever-lasting covenant, to be God to you and to your descendants after you' (Gen. xvii. 7). This promise is fulfilled in the Sinai events, through the setting up of the tent of meeting and all its furnishings, the ordination of the Aaronid priesthood and the legitimate sacrifice which, according to Leviticus ix, God accepts by his theophany and the sending of fire. The promise is fulfilled through certain permanent institutions, through which Israel becomes Yahweh's people and Yahweh becomes the God of Israel.

Why was this revolutionary reworking of the older view of Israel's history made by the Priestly Document? It is clear that, at an earlier stage, the Priestly tradition also spoke of a covenant in the time of Moses. Thus, for instance, the final chapter of the Holiness Code mentions the sword which executes vengeance for the covenant, in describing the curse upon the disobedient. In Exodus xxxi. 17 the sabbath is mentioned as a sign which points to the covenant as its original background. Through the bold alteration made by the Priestly Document the whole covenant relationship of Israel becomes anchored in the Abraham covenant. Thus it is rooted in a covenant which contains no proclamation of law, but is a complete gift, proclaiming an election of grace. The sword of vengeance no longer has any place here. Thus, according to the Priestly Document, Moses proclaimed no apodic-tic law. The two tablets which Moses received on the mountain are mentioned only incidentally, and they are referred to as 'the tablets of the testimony' (Exod. xxxi. 18). They no longer have any threatening power, but have become a sacramental guarantee.

In the prophets we heard the proclamation of a new coming of God in order to establish a covenant, or of a betrothal, or simply of a gift which finally removes the danger of the curse of the law, by giving the

---

[1] Cf. my essay, 'Sinaibund und Abrahambund', *ThZ* 16, 1960, pp. 268–280, reprinted in *Gottes Offenbarung*, pp. 205–16.

power for true obedience and a new heart by God's spirit. The Priestly Document makes no mention of the prophetic hope. By revising the older view of Israel's history in a new theological construction it seeks to make clear that God's people are wholly founded on his gracious will. The removal of the Mosaic covenant from the theology of the Priestly Document shows, as does the preaching of Deutero-Isaiah, that both the prophetic preaching of judgment upon disobedience to God's law, and the execution of this judgment in the exile, have passed.

We must end our discussion here. We began with the striking summary by which the New Testament refers to the Old Testament canon as 'the Law and the Prophets'. We have seen something of the tension which lies behind these two entities. The problem which was contained in the old covenant law of Israel was brought into the open by the prophets. They announced that the covenant with Israel could not remain static, but must await its fulfilment. They announced with certainty that God was in course of accomplishing this fulfilment, and that the curse, which hovered over the divine law as a hidden threat, would be robbed of its power.

With this we reach the point at which we encounter the testimony of the faithful servant, Jesus the Christ of Israel. When the time was fulfilled (Gal. iv. 4), he took the curse upon himself, and bore the sin of many. The discussion of this falls, however, outside the scope of this study.

Postscript

THE title 'the Law and the Prophets' has served us as a guide through the preceding chapters. This path at first led through the history of Old Testament scholarship, and then brought us directly to the heart of the message of the Old Testament. At this point another path became visible. 'The Law and the Prophets' not only designate two forms of Old Testament thinking, but they also represent two successive stages of a development. The outcome of this development is by no means an established fact. The peculiarity of Old Testament history lies in the fact that the preacher accompanies the events, making God's word audible in them. God speaks to his people in history, and this word is always seeking to be heard. This word, however, is never simply an idea, whether of morality or of theology, but is rather an event, which cannot be separated from other historical events in Israel. The law (*torah*) in Israel did not exist apart from the event of Israel's liberation from the house of bondage in Egypt (Exod. xx. 2). Similarly the prophets had no reality apart from the judgment and death which took place in the exile.

Our path from the law to the prophets was a path by which the tension already inherent in the Old Testament law, entered into the very history of Israel. Israel lived through the call of its God, by which the holy and zealous Lord (Exod. xx. 5) turned to his people in mercy. This is the *kerygma* of the Old Testament, and it bears witness to the 'truth' of it in terms of a historical event.

With the preaching of the prophets, and the historical events which accompanied it, Israel's confidence in the firmness of their foundations was shaken, and the people were confronted with an unknown and uncertain future. They became a people awaiting the fullness of their life through an event which had not yet taken place. The prophets proclaimed that a new act of God was necessary to show that the holy and zealous Lord would really uphold his people, since the law had revealed their complete inability to obey his will. Their message promised that this divine act would take place, surpassing all human possibilities, and by it God would create a new obedience in man. They promised life to a people under judgment.

Quite apart from the preaching of the prophets, Israel was already well aware of the fact that it owed its life entirely to the promise of God. The first book of the *torah*, Genesis, describes how God gave his promise to the patriarchs, assuring them of the growth of their descendants into a nation, and adding to this the promise of possession of the land of Canaan. At the end of our final chapter we mentioned very briefly the later expansion of this promise in the Priestly Document. The prophets were aware of the hopeless condition of sinful Israel before its holy and zealous God, and by their preaching they sought to reawaken a faith in the divine promise. In their message this faith became more profound and intense, and its content was remoulded, and related to the future in a new way. Israel could only live by the grace of God, and the prophets declared that God would come to complete his work of salvation, and ultimately he would enable his people to be completely obedient. Thus, in the preaching of the prophets, Israel became a people of hope and anticipation. The early post-exilic prophets, Haggai, Zechariah and Trito-Isaiah show that the return from exile was in no way to be understood as the real fulfilment of the prophetic promise.

After the later apocaplytic theology of the inter-testamental period, the New Testament witness to the coming of the Christ was made in the context of this hope. The apostles recognized the fulfilment of the Old Testament hope in the astonishing historical encounter with Jesus of Nazareth, his message of the Kingdom of God, his crucifixion and resurrection. The Old Testament provided for them the true and interpretative explanation of the Christ event. This is perfectly clear in the early Christian confession of faith, as is shown by Paul's references in 1 Corinthians xv. 3 f.; Romans iii. 21, and also in Luke xxiv. 25–27, 44. In the crucifixion of Jesus the earliest Christians saw one who had submitted to the curse of the law, and who, by taking this curse upon himself, made possible something new. In the gift of the Holy Spirit, Christians were summoned to the new freedom of the children of God, through the message of the crucified and risen Jesus, and thus they enjoyed the first fulfilment of the promised new creation. In this mighty act of divine love, God's free grace was the first and final reality. The first Christians, therefore, could not close their eyes to the revolutionary fact that this message was sent into all the world, calling both Jews and Greeks, and thus more than fulfilled the promise of Deutero-Isaiah. The Gospel made it possible for the prerogatives of Israel as a nation to become the prerogatives of a great brotherhood.

In this fact Christian theology is given its task. It must examine whether the interpretation of Jesus of Nazareth as the Christ, to which the Old Testament testifies, is legitimate. In doing so it must not regard the Old Testament in a literalistic fashion as a book of 'oracles', but must rather seek to uncover the heart of the divine promise, such as became visible in our discussion of 'the Law and the Prophets'. The prophetic message does not point us to the expectation of a simple event which could be described and predicted like an oracle, but to the expectation of a full revelation of God in the people he has called by his grace. Immanuel—'God with us', the presence of the holy God whose justice is incorruptible, is the theme of the prophets, as of the Old Testament as a whole.

This points the way to the varied tasks of Christian scholarship. Old Testament research must direct its efforts towards obtaining a knowledge and understanding of the divine promise and *kerygma* given in the Old Testament. In this connection everything that has been recently learned about the historical uniqueness of the Old Testament must be considered. The central message of the Old Testament is not the discovery of the idea of monotheism, or the realization of a higher morality, nor even the arrival of a timeless 'fundamental promise', as F. Baumgärtel argues.[1] It is rather to be found in an understanding of certain historical events as an expression of divine grace and judgment. The proclamation of these events leads on to an expectation of a further coming act of God.

New Testament scholarship must inquire how far the Christ proclaimed in the apostolic preaching may be understood as the fulfilment of the Old Testament. It is to him, as God's final revelation, that all faith is directed. Scholarship must ask in what sense the act of divine grace in Christ is valid 'once and for all', and how in his person 'God with us' appears in judgment and salvation. What does the New Testament mean when it proclaims Christ as the one who has come in fulfilment of God's promise to Israel?

Systematic theology must determine the significance of all this for the unfolding of the Christian faith and its knowledge of God. It must inquire into its meaning for the form of Christian love, and the character of the Christian hope, showing that God's love is manifested in an event of fulfilled promise, and that Christ came to a people called to wait and hope, by the word of God manifested in history. This is the decisive defence against any gnostic understanding of the love of God.

[1] F. BAUMGÄRTEL, *Verheissung. Zur Frage des evangelischen Verständnisses des Alten Testaments*, Gütersloh, 1952.

It secures the truly historical understanding of God's faithfulness, which has continued from the past to the present, and which will continue from the present to the future. God's faithfulness is not revealed to man as an unreal, timeless being, but to a real man, who is on the way from yesterday to tomorrow.

In all of this, however, a dialogue with Judaism becomes inevitable. Judaism has stood its ground throughout the centuries, momentous as they have been, through faith in God's faithful word, from which it has regarded it as necessary to exclude the name of Jesus Christ. If we take 'the Law and the Prophets' as true witnesses to the living God, who announce his coming to his people, then the open, brotherly and listening conversation of the Church with Israel is no longer a matter of mere goodwill. The question of the validity of the divine demand and promise, contained in 'the Law and the Prophets', then becomes one of burning importance.

Authors

Biblical References

98

harper 🔥 torchbooks

HUMANITIES AND SOCIAL SCIENCES

American Studies: General

CARL N. DEGLER, Ed.: Pivotal Interpretations of American History   TB/1240, TB/1241
A. S. EISENSTADT, Ed.: The Craft of American History Vol. I TB/1255; Vol. II TB/1256
CHARLOTTE P. GILMAN: Women and Economics § TB/3073
JOHN HIGHAM, Ed.: The Reconstruction of American History △   TB/1068
JOHN F. KENNEDY: A Nation of Immigrants △ TB/1118
LEONARD W. LEVY, Ed.: American Constitutional Law   TB/1285
ARNOLD ROSE: The Negro in America   TB/3048

American Studies: Colonial

BERNARD BAILYN, Ed.: The Apologia of Robert Keayne: Self-Portrait of a Puritan Merchant   TB/1201
LAWRENCE HENRY GIPSON: The Coming of the Revolution: 1763-1775. † Illus.   TB/3007
PERRY MILLER & T. H. JOHNSON, Eds.: The Puritans: A Sourcebook   Vol. I TB/1093; Vol. II TB/1094
EDMUND S. MORGAN, Ed.: The Diary of Michael Wigglesworth, 1653-1657   TB/1228
EDMUND S. MORGAN: The Puritan Family   TB/1227
RICHARD B. MORRIS: Government and Labor in Early America   TB/1244
WALLACE NOTESTEIN: The English People on the Eve of Colonization: 1603-1630. † Illus.   TB/3006

American Studies: From the Revolution to 1860

RAY A. BILLINGTON: The Far Western Frontier: 1830-1860. † Illus.   TB/3012
W. R. BROCK: An American Crisis: Congress and Reconstruction, 1865-67 º △   TB/1283
GEORGE DANGERFIELD: The Awakening of American Nationalism: 1815-1828. † Illus.   TB/3061
RICHARD B. MORRIS, Ed.: The Era of the American Revolution   TB/1180
A. F. TYLER: Freedom's Ferment   TB/1074

American Studies: Since the Civil War

MAX BELOFF, Ed.: The Debate on the American Revolution, 1761-1783: A Sourcebook △   TB/1225
EDMUND BURKE: On the American Revolution. † Edited by Elliot Robert Barkan   TB/3068
WHITNEY R. CROSS: The Burned-Over District: The Social and Intellectual History of Enthusiastic Religion in Western New York, 1800-1850   TB/1242
W. A. DUNNING: Reconstruction, Political and Economic: 1865-1877   TB/1073
FRANCIS GRIERSON: The Valley of Shadows   TB/1246
SIDNEY HOOK: Reason, Social Myths, and Democracy   TB/1237

WILLIAM E. LEUCHTENBURG: Franklin D. Roosevelt and the New Deal: 1932-1940. † Illus.   TB/3025
ARTHUR S. LINK: Woodrow Wilson and the Progressive Era: 1910-1917. † Illus.   TB/3023
JAMES MADISON: The Forging of American Federalism. Edited by Saul K. Padover   TB/1226
ROBERT GREEN MC CLOSKEY: American Conservatism in the Age of Enterprise: 1865-1910   TB/1137
ARTHUR MANN: Yankee Reformers in the Urban Age   TB/1247
GEORGE E. MOWRY: The Era of Theodore Roosevelt and the Birth of Modern America: 1900-1912. † TB/3022
R. B. NYE: Midwestern Progressive Politics   TB/1202
FRANCIS S. PHILBRICK: The Rise of the West, 1754-1830. † Illus.   TB/3067
WILLIAM PRESTON, JR.: Aliens and Dissenters TB/1287
JACOB RIIS: The Making of an American ‡   TB/3070
PHILIP SELZNICK: TVA and the Grass Roots: A Study in the Sociology of Formal Organization   TB/1230
TIMOTHY L. SMITH: Revivalism and Social Reform: American Protestantism on the Eve of the Civil War   TB/1229
IDA M. TARBELL: The History of the Standard Oil Company. Briefer Version. ‡ Edited by David M. Chalmers   TB/3071
GEORGE B. TINDALL, Ed.: A Populist Reader ‡ TB/3069
ALBION W. TOURGÉE: A Fool's Errand   TB/3074
VERNON LANE WHARTON: The Negro in Mississippi: 1865-1890   TB/1178

Anthropology

JACQUES BARZUN: Race: A Study in Superstition. Revised Edition   TB/1172
JOSEPH B. CASAGRANDE, Ed.: In the Company of Man: Portraits of Anthropological Informants.   TB/3047
DAVID LANDY: Tropical Childhood: Cultural Transmission and Learning in a Puerto Rican Village ¶ TB/1235
EDWARD BURNETT TYLOR: The Origins of Culture. Part I of "Primitive Culture." § Intro. by Paul Radin TB/33
EDWARD BURNETT TYLOR: Religion in Primitive Culture. Part II of "Primitive Culture" §   TB/34
W. LLOYD WARNER: A Black Civilization: A Study of an Australian Tribe. ¶ Illus.   TB/3056

Art and Art History

EMILE MÂLE: The Gothic Image: Religious Art in France of the Thirteenth Century. § △ 190 illus. TB/44
ERICH NEUMANN: The Archetypal World of Henry Moore. △ 107 illus.   TB/2020
DORA & ERWIN PANOFSKY: Pandora's Box: The Changing Aspects of a Mythical Symbol   TB/2021

Business, Economics & Economic History

GILBERT BURCK & EDITORS OF FORTUNE: The Computer Age: And Its Potential for Management TB/1179

---

† The New American Nation Series, edited by Henry Steele Commager and Richard B. Morris.
‡ American Perspectives series, edited by Bernard Wishy and William E. Leuchtenburg.
* The Rise of Modern Europe series, edited by William L. Langer.
¶ Researches in the Social, Cultural, and Behavioral Sciences, edited by Benjamin Nelson.
§ The Library of Religion and Culture, edited by Benjamin Nelson.
Σ Harper Modern Science Series, edited by James R. Newman.
º Not for sale in Canada.
△ Not for sale in the U. K.

THOMAS C. COCHRAN: The American Business System: A
Historical Perspective, 1900-1955   TB/1080
FRANK H. KNIGHT: Risk, Uncertainty and Profit   TB/1215
ABBA P. LERNER: Everybody's Business   TB/3051
HERBERT SIMON: The Shape of Automation   TB/1245
PIERRE URI: Partnership for Progress: A Program for
Transatlantic Action   TB/3036

Historiography & Philosophy of History

JACOB BURCKHARDT: On History and Historians. △ Intro.
by H. R. Trevor-Roper   TB/1216
H. STUART HUGHES: History as Art and as Science: Twin
Vistas on the Past   TB/1207
ARNOLDO MOMIGLIANO: Studies in Historiography
TB/1288
GEORGE H. NADEL, Ed.: Studies in the Philosophy of His-
tory: Essays from History and Theory   TB/1208
KARL R. POPPER: The Open Society and Its Enemies △
Vol. I TB/1101; Vol. II TB/1102
KARL R. POPPER: The Poverty of Historicism ० △ TB/1126
G. J. RENIER: History: Its Purpose and Method △ TB/1209
W. H. WALSH: Philosophy of History △   TB/1020

History: General

L. CARRINGTON GOODRICH: A Short History of the Chi-
nese People. △ Illus.   TB/3015
DAN N. JACOBS & HANS H. BAERWALD: Chinese Commu-
nism: Selected Documents   TB/3031
BERNARD LEWIS: The Arabs in History △   TB/1029
BERNARD LEWIS: Middle East and West ० △   TB/1274

History: Ancient and Medieval

HELEN CAM: England before Elizabeth △   TB/1026
NORMAN COHN: The Pursuit of the Millennium △ TB/1037
CHRISTOPHER DAWSON, Ed.: Mission to Asia △   TB/315
ADOLF ERMAN, Ed.: The Ancient Egyptians △   TB/1233
F. L. GANSHOF: Feudalism △   TB/1058
DENO GEANAKOPLOS: Byzantine East and Latin West △
TB/1265
DENYS HAY: Europe: Emergence of an Idea   TB/1275
DENYS HAY: The Medieval Centuries ० △   TB/1192
SAMUEL NOAH KRAMER: Sumerian Mythology   TB/1055
NAPHTALI LEWIS & MEYER REINHOLD, Eds.: Roman Civiliza-
tion   Vol. I TB/1231; Vol. II TB/1232
CHARLES PETIT-DUTAILLIS: The Feudal Monarchy in France
and England ० △   TB/1165
HENRI PIRENNE: Early Democracies in the Low Countries
TB/1110
STEVEN RUNCIMAN: A History of the Crusades. △
Vol. I TB/1143; Vol. II TB/1243

History: Renaissance & Reformation

JACOB BURCKHARDT: The Civilization of the Renaissance
in Italy △   Vol. I TB/40; Vol. II TB/41
JOHN CALVIN & JACOPO SADOLETO: A Reformation De-
bate. Edited by John C. Olin   TB/1239
G. CONSTANT: The Reformation in England △   TB/314
G. R. ELTON: Reformation Europe, 1517-1559 ० △ TB/1270
J. H. HEXTER: More's Utopia: The Biography of an Idea.
New Epilogue by the Author   TB/1195
HAJO HOLBORN: Ulrich von Hutten and the German Ref-
ormation   TB/1238
JOEL HURSTFIELD, Ed.: The Reformation Crisis △ TB/1267
ULRICH VON HUTTEN et al.: On the Eve of the Reforma-
tion. "Letters of Obscure Men." Introduction by Hajo
Holborn   TB/1124
PAUL O. KRISTELLER: Renaissance Thought: The Classic,
Scholastic, and Humanist Strains   TB/1048
ROBERT LATOUCHE: The Birth of Western Economy
TB/1290
GARRETT MATTINGLY et al.: Renaissance Profiles. △ Edited
by J. H. Plumb   TB/1162
J. E. NEALE: The Age of Catherine de Medici ० △ TB/1085
ERWIN PANOFSKY: Studies in Iconology △   TB/1077
J. H. PLUMB: The Italian Renaissance △   TB/1161
A. F. POLLARD: Henry VIII ० △   TB/1249
A. F. POLLARD: Wolsey ० △   TB/1248

A. L. ROWSE: The Expansion of Elizabethan England. ० △
Illus.   TB/1220
G. M. TREVELYAN: England in the Age of Wycliffe, 1368-
1520 ० △   TB/1112
VESPASIANO: Renaissance Princes, Popes, and Prelates:
The Vespasiano Memoirs   TB/1111

History: Modern European

MAX BELOFF: The Age of Absolutism, 1660-1815 △
TB/1062
ASA BRIGGS: The Making of Modern England, 1784-
1867: The Age of Improvement ० △   TB/1203
CRANE BRINTON: A Decade of Revolution, 1789-1799. *
Illus.   TB/3018
D. W. BROGAN: The Development of Modern France. ० △
Vol. I TB/1184; Vol. II TB/1185
J. BRONOWSKI & BRUCE MAZLISH: The Western Intellectual
Tradition: From Leonardo to Hegel   TB/3001
ALAN BULLOCK: Hitler, A Study in Tyranny ० △ TB/1123
E. H. CARR: German-Soviet Relations Between the Two
World Wars, 1919-1939   TB/1278
E. H. CARR: International Relations Between the Two
World Wars, 1919-1939 ० △   TB/1279
E. H. CARR: The Twenty Years' Crisis, 1919-1939 ० △
TB/1122
GORDON A. CRAIG: Bismarck to Adenauer   TB/1171
FRANKLIN L. FORD: Robe and Sword: The Regrouping of
the French Aristocracy after Louis XIV   TB/1217
RENÉ FUELOEP-MILLER: The Mind and Face of Bolshe-
vism   TB/1188
HANS KOHN, Ed.: The Mind of Modern Russia   TB/1065
WALTER LAQUEUR & GEORGE L. MOSSE, Eds.: International
Fascism, 1920-1945 ० △   TB/1276
WALTER LAQUEUR & GEORGE L. MOSSE, Eds.: Left-Wing
Intelligentsia Between the Two World Wars   TB/1286
FRANK E. MANUEL: The Prophets of Paris: Turgot, Con-
dorcet, Saint-Simon, Fourier, and Comte   TB/1218
L. B. NAMIER: Facing East △   TB/1280
L. B. NAMIER: Personalities and Powers △   TB/1186
FRANZ NEUMANN: Behemoth   TB/1289
DAVID OGG: Europe of the Ancien Régime, 1715-1783 ० △
TB/1271
PENFIELD ROBERTS: The Quest for Security, 1715-1740. *
Illus.   TB/3016
GEORGE RUDÉ: Revolutionary Europe, 1783-1815 ० △
TB/1272
LOUIS, DUC DE SAINT-SIMON: Versailles, The Court, and
Louis XIV △   TB/1250
A. J. P. TAYLOR: From Napoleon to Lenin: Historical Es-
says ० △   TB/1268
A. J. P. TAYLOR: The Habsburg Monarchy, 1809-1918 ० △
TB/1187
G. M. TREVELYAN: British History in the Nineteenth
Century and After: 1782-1919 △   TB/1251
H. R. TREVOR-ROPER: Historical Essays ० △   TB/1269
ELIZABETH WISKEMANN: Europe of the Dictators, 1919-
1945 ० △   TB/1273

Intellectual History & History of Ideas

ERNST CASSIRER: The Individual and the Cosmos in
Renaissance Philosophy. △ Translated with an Introduction by Mario Domandi   TB/1097
FRANK E. MANUEL: The Prophets of Paris: Turgot, Con-
dorcet, Saint-Simon, Fourier, and Comte   TB/1218
PHILIP P. WIENER: Evolution and the Founders of Prag-
matism. △ Foreword by John Dewey   TB/1212

Literature, Poetry, The Novel & Criticism

JAMES BOSWELL: The Life of Dr. Johnson & The Journal
of a Tour to the Hebrides with Samuel Johnson
LL.D.: Selections ० △   TB/1254
RICHMOND LATTIMORE: The Poetry of Greek Tragedy △
TB/1257
J. B. LEISHMAN: The Monarch of Wit: An Analytical
and Comparative Study of the Poetry of John
Donne ० △   TB/1258